# SER~~~~
# WILL~~~~

A LIFE STORY

## Sarah Shephard
### Illustrated by Sarah Papworth

SCHOLASTIC

Published in the UK by Scholastic Children's Books, 2021
Euston House, 24 Eversholt Street, London, NW1 1DB

A division of Scholastic Limited
London – New York – Toronto – Sydney – Auckland
Mexico City – New Delhi – Hong Kong

Text © Sarah Shephard, 2021
Illustrations by Sarah Papworth

The right of Sarah Shephard to be identified as the author of this
work has been asserted by them in accordance with the Copyright, Designs
and Patents Act, 1988.

ISBN 978 0702 30284 8

Printed and bound by CPI Group (UK) Ltd, Croydon, CR0 4YY

Papers used by Scholastic Children's Books are made from wood grown in
sustainable forests.

1 3 5 7 9 10 8 6 4 2

www.scholastic.co.uk

# CONTENTS

# INTRODUCTION

Long after the crowds had gone home, the television and radio broadcasters had packed away their equipment and the officials had clocked off, there was an unusual sight on the main tennis court of Auckland's ASB Arena.

Serena Williams was doing cartwheels along the baseline.

Yes, Serena Williams. The winner of twenty-three Grand Slam titles had just picked up a seventy-third trophy to add to her collection and was celebrating in true Serena fashion.

The New Zealand tournament itself is not a particularly big or well-known one, but winning it marked one of Serena's greatest achievements (though there have been many of those, as you will soon discover).

Why was it such a big deal? Well, timing for one. The tournament took place in January 2020, which was twenty-five years after Serena played her very first professional tennis tournament, just a few months after she turned fourteen. Winning meant she had lifted trophies in each of the last four decades – the 1990s, 2000s, 2010s and 2020s.

The second reason it was such an important win was because it was Serena's first in three years. Since the 2017 Australian Open she had been busy starting a family of her own, giving birth to daughter Alexis Olympia Ohanian Jr in September 2017 and marrying Alexis Ohanian two months later, in November.

Serena, Alex and Olympia

Many people had doubted whether Serena would ever play tennis at the top level again. After all, she was in her late thirties by then. Most top players have retired by that age.

But those doubters clearly didn't know Serena.

She's never been the kind of person to back down from a challenge. In fact, challenges only make her more determined to succeed.

They always have done.

To find out why, we have to go way back to the beginning. To a time when Serena's determination was focused on one simple goal: to be just like her big sister, Venus.

# LOTTERY WINNERS

**W**hen the people of Compton saw the grubby yellow Volkswagen minibus with the white roof roll up to the local park, they knew exactly what was about to happen. For the next couple of hours, the tennis courts belonged to the Williams family, just as they did every day from around three o' clock in the afternoon once school finished. And some days from six in the morning too, so the girls could clock up some court time before school even started.

*Volkswagen minibus*

There were five Williams sisters in total: Yetunde (Tunde for short) was the eldest, followed by Isha, Lyndrea (who they all called Lyn), Venus, and the baby of them all, Serena, who was often called Meeka (a shortened version of her middle name Jameka).

And the reason these five kids were so dedicated to a sport they had only ever really seen played on television or behind the wire fences of the nearest country club? That was their father, Richard Williams. Not because he'd grown up in a family of tennis champions or had been a particularly good player himself, but because before Venus and Serena were even born, he decided that they were going to become the best tennis players in the world.

That's right: before they were born.

It's a story that has become just as famous as his world-beating daughters: that one day, Richard Williams was flicking around television channels when he settled on one showing a women's tennis match featuring Romanian tennis player, and winner of the 1978 French Open, Virginia Ruzici. He was captivated by the way she played – it was a style that had both beauty and risk to it.

But his captivation soon turned to astonishment. At the end of the match the commentator explained that Ruzici had won $40,000 for four days of tournament play. It was more money than Richard earned in an entire year running his security business.

That was the moment he decided that tennis would be the way forward for the Williams family, which at that time consisted of the three oldest girls: Yetunde, Isha and Lyndrea.

"We need to make two more kids and make them into tennis superstars," he said to his wife, Oracene.

He might as well have said: "We need to win the lottery this year... Actually, we need to win it twice!"

Think about how difficult it is for a parent to see even one child reach the very top level of their chosen sport. Now think about how difficult it is for a parent to see two of their children do that.

But Richard was determined. To understand why, it helps to know a little about his life up to this point.

Richard
Williams

Richard Williams was born into a life of poverty. He was raised by his mother Julia Mae Williams in a place called Shreveport, Louisiana, where he and his four sisters grew up in a three-bedroom shack next to the railroad tracks. There was no indoor toilet, just an outhouse in the back garden, and the roof was dotted with so many holes that a lake would appear inside the shack every time it rained.

At that time in the 1940s, segregation was common in America and racism was rife, particularly in southern states like Louisiana. In

Shreveport, a quiet little city in the north-western part of the state, Black people and white people were separated at every turn: in restaurants, cinemas, parks, hotels and public toilets. Violence towards young Black men was common.

Richard's childhood was spent working hard to help his mother. He got his first job at the age of five, sweeping the office of a local doctor every day before school. At eight, he was also cleaning the bottom of oil tanks after school. And by nine, he was digging holes for the Louisiana Fence Company.

When he wasn't at work or at school, Richard was simply trying to survive the dangers that seemed to lurk around every corner. He couldn't avoid them all though. One day, he was held down by a group of white men who drove a metal spike into his leg, simply because he refused to call them "Mister". On another occasion, he accidentally touched the hand of a white shop owner when paying for a chocolate bar, forgetting that Black children were supposed to place their money on the counter. His punishment was two heavy blows from a stick smashed across his back.

All these experiences only made him tougher. As did the lessons passed on by his mother Julia, a wise, strong woman who taught her son to live by the principles of courage, confidence, commitment, faith and love – the same ones he would later pass on to his daughters.

## SEGREGATION

- After slavery was made illegal in America in 1865, many people believed that Black and white Americans could not and should not coexist.
- The country embarked on a path of legally mandated segregation which meant there were separate facilities, services and opportunities available to people depending on their race.
- Black people weren't allowed to live, work or go to school in certain places. There were even certain areas of buses and trains where they were not allowed to sit.

• In 1964 the Civil Rights Act was signed, outlawing discrimination. In reality, it took many years after that for desegregation to be fully implemented.

By the time he met Oracene Price, Richard had left Shreveport and moved to Compton in California. He was tired of working for other people and thought that California would offer him more opportunities.

But before he could do that, Richard had to earn some money. He got a job working in the post room of a bank and after several years also enrolled at business school. Both of those experiences helped to put in place the groundwork for what would eventually become his own business.

Richard was familiar with the maintenance company that provided staff to clean the bank each night and saw an opportunity to start up a maintenance company. In 1967 he created the White Glove Maintenance Corporation and before long, it was bringing in almost four thousand dollars a month. But it wasn't satisfying his ambitions.

In the mid-seventies, Richard sold the company for a handsome profit and moved into the cement business. He would buy cement from construction jobs and paving companies, and sell it on to companies building new homes.

Still, he didn't feel as though he had found the business that was going to get him to where he really wanted to be – in one of the grand houses he saw in an area called Glendale where homes were worth somewhere between $150,000 and $200,000. He had come a long way from Shreveport, but still believed there was more to come. Much more.

Many people saw nothing but trouble in the run-down, crime-ridden city of Compton situated to the south of downtown Los Angeles. Richard saw nothing but opportunity. He noted the endless stream of robberies leaving businesses out of pocket, and lack of faith that people had in the police and started his own security firm.

Samson Security Service soon had a staff of more than fifty and contracts to look after several of the banks, office buildings and construction sites in Compton.

It was just as well because, before he knew it, Richard had a family of his own to look after.

Oracene Price was waiting at a bus stop in the summer of 1978 when Richard happened to drive past. Something about her caught his eye and he drove right around the block just so he could go back and speak to her.

She was from the state of Michigan, but worked as a nurse in LA. Richard liked that she was educated and mirrored his ambitious nature. He later found out she had three daughters from a previous relationship and was raising them alone, just as his own mother had done with him and his sisters. It didn't take long for the pair to fall in love and make plans to marry. Richard got on well with her three young daughters: Yetunde, Isha and Lyndrea, and grew to love them as if they were his own.

Together, the five of them moved into a house in Long Beach just a few minutes' walk from the ocean. It was there on one sunny Sunday afternoon in the late 1970s that their lives changed course for ever.

Richard was watching television with his daughters and flicking through the channels to find something they could all watch. Suddenly, something caught his attention. It was a women's tennis match. Actually, it was the end of a women's tennis match, and they had tuned in just in time to see the winner, Virginia Ruzici, picking up a cheque for $40,000.

"That's not bad for four days' work," the commentator said, chuckling. Richard was astonished. He hadn't thought it was possible for anyone to earn such an amount of money in that space of time, let alone a woman.

## THE WOMEN'S TENNIS ASSOCIATION (WTA)

• When tennis turned professional in 1968 (also called the start of the Open Era) there was a huge difference between how much women were able to earn from playing the game compared to men. At the first Open Wimbledon the winner of the women's singles title, Billie Jean King, won £750 while the men's champion, Rod Laver, took home £2,000.

• Some tournaments also started to become "Men Only", meaning female players had fewer opportunities to play.

• As one of the top female players at the time Billie Jean King decided to do something about it. In 1970 she gathered eight other female players together at the home of World Tennis Magazine founder and editor Gladys Heldman and they agreed to set up the first women's only tournament in Houston.

• After the success of that event – the Virginia Slims Invitation – the women decided they should start their own series of tournaments, and so the Virginia Slims Series was born. It started small, but by 1973 it consisted of twenty-two US-based tournaments and offered $775,000 in prize money.

- By then, the United States Tennis Association had started their own women's tour to rival the Virginia Slims circuit. But King knew that for the female players to have real power, they needed to all be working together.

- A week before Wimbledon in the summer of 1973 King held a meeting for sixty-four top female players in a London hotel. Armed with legal documents for them all to sign, King ensured that by the time the meeting was over they were all in agreement. From now on all the professional female tennis players would compete under one banner: the Women's Tennis Association (WTA).

From then on, Richard couldn't get the thought out of his head: if he had two more daughters and made them into tennis champions, the winnings would be twice as good!

There was just one problem: Richard didn't know anything about tennis.

Scratch that. There were two problems: Richard wasn't even sure if Oracene wanted any more children.

But he was not thrown off course by such doubts. He wrote up a seventy-eight-page plan, detailing how he would turn his two daughters (who did not yet exist) into champions, and cleared the way with Oracene. She understood his desire to have children of his own, and having been a keen athlete herself as a child, she was intrigued by Richard's plan.

His next step was to learn the game. Tennis had never been a sport that interested him like basketball or American football. He didn't know anyone who played it and had always seen it as a sport played mostly by white people. He wondered why that was, and whether it might even work to his advantage.

Armed with a second-hand racquet, a mountain of used balls and as many instruction videos and books as he could lay his hands on, Richard set about learning how to play tennis. It consumed him. His mornings before work were spent on the courts at his local park, either playing with a local coach nicknamed "Old Whiskey", or simply bouncing ball after ball off a wall. And each night, he spent hours with his head stuck in books about hitting techniques and foot positions.

At first, he was terrible. He'd lose every game he played against the regulars he found on the busy courts of Lynwood Park in south LA. But with consistent, relentless practice, and hours spent analysing tape after tape of matches, he improved quickly. Within a matter of months, Richard was beating the same players who had previously dispatched him so easily.

That was lucky because, before long, daughter number one arrived. Venus Ebony Starr Williams was born on 17 June 1980. And around fifteen months later, on 26 September 1981, she was followed by her sister, Serena Jameka Williams.

Finally, Richard had his future tennis champions. And the real work was about to begin.

Althea Gibson

## THE FIRST BLACK WIMBLEDON CHAMPION

• In 1957, Althea Gibson became the first Black tennis player to win Wimbledon in the competition's eighty-year history. She was also the first champion to be awarded the trophy personally by Queen Elizabeth II, and later said that "shaking hands with the queen of England was a long way from being forced to sit in the coloured section of the bus".

• A year before her Wimbledon triumph, Gibson had become the first African-American to win a Grand Slam tournament when she won the French Open women's singles title.

• By the time she retired in late 1958, Gibson had won eleven Grand Slam titles (five singles, five doubles and one mixed doubles). And she had done it without being afforded the same privileges as her white counterparts, often sleeping in her car while travelling to tournaments around the world because she wouldn't be allowed into the hotels.

# STRAIGHT OUTTA COMPTON

Serena was not yet two years old when her dad decided that the tranquillity of Long Beach was not the right place to raise his future tennis champions. Instead, Richard moved his wife and five daughters back to Compton in South Central Los Angeles. It was a tough neighbourhood and his girls would have to grow up rough and tough enough to survive it, just like he had to growing up in Shreveport.

He bought a house on East Stockton Street where all five girls shared one bedroom. It was a tight squeeze and there was only room for four beds in there (two sets of bunk beds), which left one Williams sister as the odd one out. As the youngest, that was normally Serena. But she didn't mind. It meant that each night she got to share a bed with a different sister and build a stronger bond with each of them. Instead of feeling as if she didn't belong anywhere, she felt she belonged everywhere.

The streets of Compton were dangerous at that time. There were a lot of gangs competing for money and power, and that meant there was a lot of crime and violence. Even the tennis courts at the local park weren't safe. They were often a "hang out spot" for gang members who were up to no good.

The actual courts had been abandoned for years. They were full of cracks and weeds and there were empty beer bottles and fast-food wrappers scattered everywhere. Richard started taking care of them, sweeping up the rubbish and trying to get them into a decent state so he could begin teaching Venus how to play. He also tried to build trust with the gang members. It was the only way he would feel safe enough to bring his daughters to the court.

## COMPTON

One of the oldest cities in Los Angeles County, Compton, gained a notorious reputation during the 1980s and 1990s, becoming famous for violence between two rival gangs: the Bloods and the Crips.

In 1988, rap group NWA put the city on the map by releasing an album called *Straight Outta Compton* which chronicled the violence they had experienced on the streets of Compton. In 1990, the murder rate in the city reached a staggering high of ninety-one per 100,000 residents.

Venus was around four years old when Richard started taking her to the tennis courts. Every time they left the house Serena would try and follow. She always wanted to be where her big sister was. Eventually Richard gave in and started taking them both with him.

Venus had always been tall for her age, but Serena was tiny and holding a regulation-size racquet only made her look even smaller. But she swung that racquet as hard as she could and the words of encouragement from her dad every time she managed to hit a ball only made her more determined to keep on doing it.

It wasn't only Venus and Serena who spent time on the tennis courts; it was the whole family. Yetunde, Isha and Lyndrea had also been taught the basics – not just by their dad, but their mum too. Oracene had been learning about the game alongside Richard and would often hit with whichever girls weren't on their dad's court. It wasn't only a way for Venus and Serena to become champions; it was a way for them all to be together as a family.

And so that's how the grubby yellow Volkswagen minibus became a familiar sight. The Williams sisters would squeeze into it alongside a shopping trolley filled with hundreds of used tennis balls Richard had collected from all the country clubs in the area and a few brooms so they could sweep the courts before they played.

Those used balls played a key role in developing Serena's game. The oldest, flattest ones would barely bounce at all so her footwork, concentration and speed became all-important if she was to get her racquet on them. Her dad would tell her, "At Wimbledon the balls will bounce low, just like these, so you have to be ready."

Preparing his daughters for everything that lay ahead, in life as well as in tennis, was so important to Richard Williams. When they were just three and four years old, he would take them out delivering phone books in their local neighbourhood for money. The weighty books were almost bigger than Serena, but she was determined to help and would team up with Venus to drag each book across their neighbours' lawns and up the front steps to deliver them together.

He taught them about planning and setting out dreams and goals for themselves. And that one of the best ways to achieve them was to put them down on paper and write down how they would get there. When Serena told him one day that she wanted to be a veterinarian, her dad told her to make notes on how to become one. She read books on the subject and asked to go and see one.

Serena didn't always understand the true value of writing down her thoughts, but it built a habit in her that she used throughout her entire tennis career. During a match, you will occasionally see her take out a small book at the changeover between games. It's her match book and is filled with pointers, reminders to herself and any quotes that she thinks might inspire her during her next match.

Dreams and goals

Richard also liked to use other sports as a way of preparing Venus and Serena for life as top tennis players. From an early age, they were learning taekwondo to make them tougher and having ballet and tap-dancing lessons to help them with their balance and movement. When they got a bit older, he had them throwing American footballs from one end of the court to the other, especially before they practised their serves. It was something he'd read in one of his coaching books, and thought it was a good idea because the sharp overhead motion you need to launch the ball is almost exactly the same as the one you need to hit a powerful serve.

Away from the sport, Venus and Serena spent much of their time with their family. They didn't go to parties or spend hours on the phone to their friends. They enjoyed playing the card game Uno and putting on pretend talent shows with their sisters (Serena liked to sing the Whitney Houston song, 'Greatest Love of All').

They also spent a lot of time at Kingdom Hall, which is a place of worship for people who are Jehovah's Witnesses. Just as Christian people will go to church, Jews to synagogue and Muslims to mosque, Jehovah's Witnesses will go to meetings at Kingdom Hall.

Serena's parents both believed it was just as important for their daughters to have religion in their lives as it was for them to have education. And as Oracene had become a Jehovah's Witness when her daughters were very young, she raised them to become Witnesses too. It was a big part of their lives. Every Sunday, Tuesday and Thursday without fail they would go to meetings at Kingdom Hall to pray, study the Bible, sing and express their faith. Even tennis practice took a back seat to meetings.

## JEHOVAH'S WITNESSES

• In the late 1800s a group of Christians branched off from the main beliefs of traditional Christianity to form their own group – the Jehovah's Witnesses.

• Jehovah is the name they use for God, so being a Jehovah's Witness simply means bearing witness to Jehovah's word.

- They study the Bible and base all their main beliefs on it, but also have their own bible translation called the New World Translation.

- Jehovah's Witnesses are expected to take an active part in preaching. This means spreading the word about their religion and trying to get others to join them. They will often go door-to-door and offer to share information about being a Jehovah's Witness with people.

- They don't believe in celebrating things like Christmas or Easter. Nor do they celebrate birthdays.

Serena was six or seven when her dad started signing her up to play in local tennis leagues as part of a team with three to five other girls. Serena would often win her matches pretty easily and spend the rest of her time playing hopscotch or doing cartwheels behind the courts. She still had a lot to learn about being a good teammate and supporting the other girls.

She was already realizing how much she loved winning though. She couldn't explain why or how she knew that she wanted it more than the other girls she played with and against, but she just knew. Winning was the best feeling in the world.

When Serena was approaching her eighth birthday, her dad came home one day and said he had signed her and Venus up for a tennis clinic with the former world number one, Billie Jean King. She had won thirty-nine Grand Slam titles and was a real legend of the game. Venus and Serena were so excited about the thought of hitting with her, they immediately ran up to the wardrobe they shared with their sisters to pick out what outfit they were going to wear.

On the day of the clinic though, Serena was left sorely disappointed. When Billie came over to her court to hit with her, she got nervous. Suddenly she couldn't get a ball in – they were all going long or smashing into the net. She knew she could play so much better. When she watched how well Venus did against Billie, it only made her feel worse.

But in the days afterwards, she realized that it didn't really matter. She had got to hit with the great Billie Jean King and that was a pretty big deal. It certainly wasn't anything she should be sad about.

Billie Jean King

## BILLIE JEAN KING

• Billie Jean King saved up eight dollars to buy her own first tennis racquet after her dad suggested she give the sport a try at the age of ten. She found a way to get lessons for free on the courts of Long Beach's public parks, and from there became one of the area's most promising young players.

- In 1961, at the age of seventeen, she won her first Grand Slam title, winning the women's doubles with Karen Hantze. But it was another five years before she added the first of her twelve Grand Slam singles titles by winning Wimbledon.

- After she won the US Open in 1972 and received $15,000 less than the winner of the men's singles title, King threatened not to play in the tournament the following year unless the prize money was made equal.

- Also in 1973, King took part in an exhibition match against former world number one Bobby Riggs that was labelled "The Battle of the Sexes". The event generated huge interest and was watched by around 90 million people worldwide.

- King felt under extreme pressure to prove the quality of women's tennis and believed that losing the match would "set women's tennis back fifty years".

- On 20 September 1973, she defeated Riggs in straight sets, picking up a cheque for $100,000. *The Sunday Times* headlined it: "The drop shot and volley heard around the world."

By this time Venus, Serena and the whole Williams family had become fairly well known on the Los Angeles tennis scene. It was Venus in particular who first started attracting the headlines though. She was around eight or nine when local newspaper first wrote an article about her and how the Williams family would all train together on the public courts around town.

There weren't too many African-American tennis players around and now here was an entire family, with two young girls who looked as though they could really shake things up. Venus was really making an impression – she was the one people were really talking about.

Serena was just the younger sister. She was much smaller than Venus and so her shots didn't have the same power as her sister's. She always had to find other ways to win – new angles to hit her shots to, trying drop shots and lobs to get the better of her opponents. But whatever she did, it was never quite enough to elevate her name alongside her sister's. It was clear that Venus was the one who people were expecting to be great, not her.

They would play against each other all the time in practice, and it was usually Venus who won. Serena's only chance of beating her was to cheat and, if that's what it took to win, she didn't mind doing it. She would call Venus's shots out when they were in and insist that her own were in when they obviously weren't. As always, Venus took it all in her stride.

Young Venus and Serena

Richard was reluctant to throw them into proper tournaments at such a young age. He was happy for them to develop as people and as players before exposing them to the pressures and attention that would come with playing in junior competitions organized by the United States Tennis Association.

It soon reached the point where Venus felt she was ready. She wanted to test herself in a tournament just like the ones they'd watch on television. At first her parents stood firm. Venus was still only nine years old and they wanted to wait a little longer. But Venus, together with Serena's help – who knew that once Venus made that step it would be easier for her to do the same – wore them down.

Richard came up with a plan: if Venus could beat him in a match then she could play. Serena wasn't sure. How would Venus beat their dad – a fully-grown man who was so much stronger and knew so much about the game that they were still learning?

On the evening that was set aside for the match, the whole family went to the park to watch and they weren't disappointed. It was a close game that left them both sweating by the end. But it was Venus who came out on top!

She and Serena were both so excited. Finally, Venus would be able to test out her game against some of the best girls in the country and Serena was sure that, before too long, she would be able to do exactly the same.

For the next six months or so, the family would be right alongside Venus as she travelled around to various tournaments, and Serena watched on wondering when her time would come. She had always wanted to be like her big sister: Venus's favourite colour was her favourite colour. Her favourite animal was Serena's favourite animal. If Venus ordered first in a restaurant, Serena wanted whatever she was having.

Now, Serena wanted to play in tournaments too. But every time she raised the subject with her dad, she'd get the same response: "Not yet, Meeka. You're not ready."

So, Serena took matters into her own hands. One afternoon not long after her eighth birthday, she found an entry form for an age-ten-and-under tournament that she knew Venus had already entered. Serena filled it in with her own details and left it in the mailbox for the postman to collect the next day. She didn't have a chequebook to include the entry fee, but decided she could deal with that when the time came.

When the day of the tournament came around, Serena got in the car with her parents and sisters armed with her racquet bag, just as she always did. There were often opportunities to hit with other kids or even with her parents in between Venus's matches, so it wasn't unusual for her to take a racquet along.

While Venus went to play her first match accompanied by the rest of the family, Serena wandered off, making her way to the registration table so she could tell the organizers she was there and ready to play. A short while later, there she was, facing her opponent, doing whatever she could to make this older, stronger girl run all over the court. She was so focused, she didn't even notice when her dad showed up.

Venus had won her match pretty easily, so Richard had started to wonder where Serena had disappeared to. When someone pointed him in the direction of one of the match courts, he was baffled. But he watched his youngest daughter play and saw that she was holding her own. In fact, she was doing more than that. She was winning.

As Serena walked off court, her dad congratulated her from the other side of the fence, telling her she played a great match and he was proud of her. Serena had been expecting some sort of punishment for entering without telling him, but he was just so happy that both his girls had won and immediately started talking about things he noticed that she could work on for her next match.

Fortunately, Serena had ended up on the other side of the draw to Venus, so she wouldn't have to worry about playing her. Unless, they both made it to the final...

Which, of course, they did. It would be the first time of many that Venus and Serena would meet in a tournament and this time, Serena knew there would be no chance of getting away with any shenanigans. There would be too many people watching.

Before the match, Richard and Oracene simply told them both to have fun, play good tennis and make sure they learned something from the experience. It was hard for them, but they knew that watching their daughters go head-to-head was something they might have to get used to over the coming years.

It was Venus who came out on top that day, winning 6–2, 6–2. But Serena had been the youngest player at the tournament and shown that she was more than capable of beating other girls of Venus's age – except for Venus herself. Even so, she was eight years old and not quite old enough to appreciate that aspect of her day. As she watched Venus get awarded the gold trophy, she looked at her silver one and wished that she had won the match.

Venus could see the disappointment in her little sister's face. She told Serena that she had always preferred silver to gold anyway and asked if she wanted to trade trophies. She made Serena feel as if it were she who would be doing her big sister the favour, not the other way around. Without a second's thought, Serena accepted the offer and took the gold trophy home. It's one she still treasures as a reminder that she has the best big sister she could ever ask for.

# SISTERS ARE DOING
# IT FOR THEMSELVES

From that day on Richard did whatever he could to make sure Venus and Serena didn't compete against each other in a tournament. He would enter Venus into events for twelve-and-unders and Serena into the ten-and-unders, ensuring that both daughters had their opportunity to shine.

But it was still Venus who was the most talked-about Williams. She was so tall that even at the age of ten she could get from one side of the court to the other in three big strides. She moved like an athlete too. That made it almost impossible for any opponent to get the ball past her.

Serena, meanwhile, was still small for her age. To win points she had to be smarter than her opponents, making them move from one side of the court to the other by playing the ball into the right areas.

Richard was happy with how they were progressing, but he started to feel as though they all needed a change. He knew that Florida had great tennis facilities and would provide an even better level of competition for Venus and Serena. Plus, Compton was still not the safest place to live and with his older daughters reaching an age where they were becoming more independent, he thought a move away from the area might be best for all of them.

It was a big move though. Florida is all the way on the other side of the country from California – a flight of about five hours, or as the Williams family later discovered a forty-hour drive! So, before they made any decisions, Richard got in touch with a few tennis coaches who ran academies in Florida to see if any of them might be a good fit for Venus and Serena.

One of the coaches who came to see them in Compton was called Rick Macci. He had heard about Venus, but wanted to see her play for himself. After all, he had some of the best kids in the country in his academy in Florida, including Jennifer Capriati, who had recently turned

**45**

professional a few weeks shy of her fourteenth birthday.

Rick flew out to Compton and met up with Richard, Venus and Serena. It was a meeting he would always remember, partly because of his surprise at finding them playing on worn out courts, scattered with broken glass. He watched Venus hit for a while and thought she looked pretty good, but perhaps not quite as special as he'd heard others suggest. Rick was a hard man to impress given the standard of kids he had in his academy.

Rick Macci

But then Venus asked her dad if she could be excused to go to the toilet. When he said yes, she dropped her racquet and playfully started handstand walking and cartwheeling her way across the court. Rick watched as she did so, his eyes widening in appreciation of what he was seeing.

He turned back to Richard and told him that if Venus worked on her strokes, he could have the next Michael Jordan on his hands. Richard pointed to Serena who'd been sitting patiently at the side of the court and replied that, actually, he had the next two.

Recognized as one of the greatest basketball players of all time, Michael Jordan spent fifteen seasons in the National Basketball Association (NBA), winning six championships with the Chicago Bulls. He became famed for his leaping ability – something that earned him the nicknames "Air Jordan" and "His Airness", and later led to the creation of the Air Jordan brand and a logo depicting his mid-jump silhouette.

Richard liked what Rick Macci had to say and it was clear from the photographs that his academy had facilities that far outshone those that Venus and Serena had been used to. Most importantly, Rick agreed with the idea of Richard coming on board as one of the coaches at the academy, meaning he would still be largely responsible for his daughters' training. After putting in so much work to get them to this point, he was not about to step aside and let someone else take over.

So, the whole family packed up and made the extremely long drive across the country to Florida. Well, it was not quite the whole family. Serena's oldest sister, Yetunde, had already moved out of home and started university by then, so she decided to stay in Los Angeles.

The Williams family settled in a place called Haines City, close to the Grenelefe resort where Rick's academy was based. It was a quiet area, which suited them just fine. School, tennis and Kingdom Hall were all Venus and Serena really had time for anyway.

They had been put on an accelerated school schedule which meant that each day they were out on the tennis court by 1 p.m. and would spend the next four or five hours working on their game. After that they'd often be at a dance class or karate lesson – whatever Richard felt would help with their tennis at that time. On Tuesdays and Thursdays they were at Kingdom Hall.

Their one day off from tennis was Sunday, when they could catch up on schoolwork and go to Kingdom Hall.

Even though their dad was still involved in their coaching, training at the academy was quite different to what Venus and Serena had been used to. There was a lot more fitness work for a start – a lot of running and even some weight training. They were also hitting more with guys than they were with girls – something that Richard believed would help to add pace and power to their game.

There was one thing in particular that separated Venus and Serena from a lot of the other kids at the academy. Many of them would spend a lot of time (and money) travelling all over the country to compete in junior tournaments, but Richard decided that Venus and Serena would be better off concentrating on school and having a bit more of a "normal" life. He'd seen the pressure that playing on the junior circuit put on some other kids and didn't think his daughters needed that at their age. Besides, Venus had already won a fair number of those tournaments before the move to Florida. What would she gain by winning even more?

His decision was met with criticism from some. How would Venus and Serena possibly be prepared for the mental and physical strains of competing on the senior WTA Tour if they never played on the junior circuit? It was the way everyone else did it, after all. But Richard stood firm. He had done things his way from the start and believed it was the best approach for his daughters.

His focus on education was so strong that whenever he felt Venus or Serena's grades weren't good enough, he would pull them off court to spend more time studying instead. Tennis would always come second to two things: his daughters' happiness and their education.

A couple of years after the Williams family moved to Florida, Rick Macci moved his academy from Grenelefe to Delray Beach. But instead of following, Richard, Oracene and their four daughters moved to a place called Pompano Beach where they went back to playing on public courts just as they had in California. From time to time they would also go to the nearby academy run by famous tennis coach Nick Bollettieri, but mostly it was Venus, Serena and their mum and dad, working towards the same dream as always: becoming the two best tennis players in the world.

Serena found the adjustment challenging.

Going from playing on the plush courts of Rick Macci's academy to sharing public courts once again took some getting used to. Their move coincided with a period where she and Venus were home-schooled by their mum – something Serena also struggled with. She enjoyed learning in a classroom atmosphere and, while her mum was a great teacher (Oracene had spent some time as a teacher before becoming a nurse), Serena found it hard to get motivated doing schoolwork at home.

But she was shaken right out of her slump towards the end of 1994 when it was decided that Venus was going to play in her first professional tournament.

It was a huge moment for the whole family. Richard had spent so long holding Venus and Serena back, but now his second youngest daughter was tugging so strongly on the reins he had to let her go. He also had to think about the new age eligibility rules that the WTA was going to impose, which would restrict the number of tournaments young players could enter and raise the age at which they could turn professional. If Venus didn't turn pro then, she could face an even longer wait.

So, in October 1994, a fourteen-year-old Venus entered the Bank of the West Classic in Oakland, California.

The tennis world couldn't wait to finally see the prodigy they'd heard so much about in action. A year earlier, twenty-four members of the worldwide media had applied for passes to attend the tournament. This time, that number rocketed up to 252. Everyone wanted to see just how good this young girl really was. Even when Venus was just hitting balls on the practice courts before her first match, the crowd watching her was three or four deep.

On the other side of the court for those practice sessions was a familiar face. The Williams family couldn't afford for all of them to travel to California to watch Venus, but Richard said Serena could go as Venus's hitting partner. She could hardly wait to get there and play alongside the top players she'd seen on television.

For Richard Williams it was a nerve-wracking day – a day they had been working towards for around nine years. He kept asking himself: what if we suddenly find out we don't belong here?

He needn't have worried. In her first-round match, Venus was up against fellow American, Shaun Stafford, who was ranked in the top sixty in the world, and it took the unranked teenager just an hour and twenty-two minutes to win 6–3, 6–4. Venus had arrived and it was obvious to everyone that she very much belonged on that court.

The only clue that she was playing at that level for the first time came during the changeovers. Richard had never let his daughters sit down during practice sessions, so Venus ignored the chair placed next to the umpire and bounced from one foot to the other to stay warm until it was time to resume play.

In her second-round match, Venus faced a much tougher task against the world number two, Arantxa Sanchez-Vicario.

Arantxa Sanchez-Vicario

But she came out hitting the ball so well that she took the first set 6–3 and then went 3–1 up in the second, before the Spanish player got herself back into the match and turned it around completely.

Venus lost the match, but she won so much besides during those few days in California, including the attention of big brands like Nike and Reebok. In the days after the tournament, Richard had phone calls from both companies enquiring about sponsoring Venus, who had worn a non-branded T-shirt and tennis skirt while playing in Oakland. In May 1995, it was Reebok who won Venus's signature on a five-year deal worth $12 million – a huge amount of money for a fourteen-year-old with just one professional tournament on her record.

That same summer, the Williams family moved to a new house in Palm Beach Gardens, meaning their practice sessions could now take place at a country club in West Palm Beach. They stopped being taught at home by their mum and started attending The Driftwood Academy, a private high school. Here, they returned to their previous regime of studying in the mornings and spending most afternoons on the tennis court.

# TENNIS SCORING

**GAMES:** The scoring system in tennis is not as straightforward as most sports. Each game starts at 0–0, which is called "love all". From there the points follow the pattern: 15, 30, 40. If two players reach 40–40 (also called "deuce") then they continue playing until one player wins two points in a row. If you win the first point after deuce, then the umpire will call your "advantage". If you win the next point after that, you have won the game. If you lose it then the score returns to deuce.

**SETS:** The first player to win six games wins the set UNLESS the score reaches five-games-all. Then there are two scenarios: if one person wins the next two games, they win the set 7–5.

If each player wins one of the next two games making it 6–6 then the set goes to a tiebreak.

**TIEBREAK:** The winner of the tiebreak is the first player to reach seven points UNLESS the score reaches 6–6. In that case, play continues until one player wins by two clear points.

**MATCH:** Most tennis matches are the best of three sets, although you will see male players play best of five sets at the Grand Slams. This was based on the outdated belief that female players would not be capable of playing best of five. Even though we now know this to be untrue, and that many female players would like to play best of five too, it has become a tradition that the tennis world finds difficult to change.

The launch of Venus on to the professional tennis scene meant there was no going back for the Williams family. They were now fully in the spotlight and Serena was desperate to grab her share of it.

A year or so after Venus's debut, Serena finally convinced her dad she was ready for hers. It came a month or so after her fourteenth birthday at the Bell Challenge in Quebec City, Canada. In her first match, Serena was up against fellow American, Annie Miller, a player ranked 149th in the world. The tournament was a smaller one than where Venus had made her debut and there was slightly less hype surrounding Serena's appearance there, but she was nervous all the same.

Less than an hour after she walked on court, Serena was trudging off it, having lost the match 6–1, 6–1. As a kid, she had been used to winning (aside from when she played Venus). Now, she had to learn that it wasn't always so easy. That she would have to fight for her victories.

Serena knew she could have played much better in Canada, but as she got older, she realized that the moment had simply been too big for her to handle at that stage. Perhaps her dad had been right all along – she was not yet ready for the professional tour.

# AFRICAN HAIR BEADS

• When Venus and Serena first started playing on the WTA Tour, they often wore their hair in braids (called cornrows) decorated with brightly coloured beads. The hairstyle dates back thousands of years and among African tribes was often used as a unique way to identify each tribe.

• Venus and Serena's mum, Oracene, said the main purpose of the beads was to show their heritage. She wanted Venus and Serena to understand where they came from and to be proud of it.

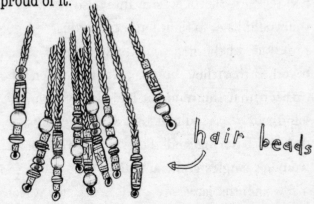

hair beads

For the next year or so, Serena went back to the practice court (and to high school). She knew that her time would come again.

In March 1997, that moment finally arrived. This time fifteen-year-old Serena would be playing at a tournament in Indian Wells, California where Venus would also be competing. But it ended in swift disappointment as Serena was beaten in her first-round match again, this time losing to world number eighty-seven Alexia Dechaume-Balleret from France – although Serena did win two more games than she had in Canada, going down 6–4, 6–0.

This time though, defeat didn't mean the end of her tournament, because Serena and Venus had entered the doubles event together.

It made a lot of sense for them to play on the same side of the net for once. It worked so well together that they made it all the way to the quarter-finals, only losing to eventual winners, Lindsay Davenport and Natasha Zvereva.

Venus also reached the quarter-finals of the women's singles at Indian Wells that year. And a few months later she made it all the way to the final of the US Open despite it being her first ever appearance at the tournament. She eventually lost to fellow teenager Martina Hingis, but it was a display that proved to everyone – including Serena – that their relative inexperience on the biggest stage was not going to prevent the Williams sisters from being a force to be reckoned with.

Not everyone was entirely welcoming of Venus's arrival at the top table of women's tennis. Some people mistook the confidence she and Serena displayed for arrogance. They were also accused of staying in such a tight-knit group together with their parents that they separated themselves from the other players on the women's tour.

A lot of it came down to the fact that Venus and Serena were different. They were sisters. They hadn't come through the "traditional" route of playing junior tennis. And they were Black. Before Venus and Serena reached the top, tennis had often seemed like a sport that was only open to certain types of people – those who had grown up around the game or had the money to join country clubs where it was played. But they were showing that tennis is a game for everyone, and it took some people a while to accept that.

Serena couldn't wait to get her own opportunity to play at a Grand Slam like Venus. But first, she had to start winning singles matches at the smaller events.

In November 1997, Serena was awarded a wild-card entry into a tournament called the Ameritech Cup in Chicago. Ranked 304th in the world, she won her first-round match against Russia's Elena Likhovsteva, setting up a second-round tie with the former Australian Open champion, Mary Pierce.

No one expected Serena to make it through to the third round, but that's exactly what she did, setting up a match against fellow American and multiple-Grand Slam winner, Monica Seles.

Once again, Serena defied all expectations to win in three sets, making such an impression on her opponent that Seles called her agent later that night and told him her days at the top were numbered. She knew she had just come up against the next great tennis champion.

Serena lost to the number three seeded player in the world, Lindsay Davenport, in the semi-finals, but there was no doubting that she had finally made her mark.

By becoming the lowest ranked player in the Open Era to defeat two top-ten ranked opponents in the same tournament she had taken a significant step towards emerging from the shadow of her big sister, Venus.

## WILD-CARD

In professional tennis, most tournaments limit their entry to players who are ranked at a certain number and above. But they also reserve a few places in the draw for wild-card entries. These are players don't have the required ranking, but whom the organizers decide deserve a spot in the tournament. In Serena's case, she was awarded one because she was a promising young player from the country hosting the tournament. A player

might also be given a wild card if they are
returning from a long-term injury.

# PRIME TIME

# "WHAT WILL YOU GIVE ME IF I WIN THE US OPEN THIS YEAR?"

**S**erena was sixteen years old when she posed this question to a man called Arnon Milchan, a billionaire Hollywood film producer who at that time also owned a stake in the Puma brand. She'd wanted her own sponsor ever since seeing Venus sign her contract with Reebok, but for a long time it seemed that no one was interested in the girl who was still known mostly as "Venus's little sister".

That was about to change.

Milchan met Richard Williams late in 1997, after buying a big chunk of the Puma brand and deciding to pursue an endorsement deal with the youngest Williams sister. They began talking and then negotiating, but Richard didn't want a deal to be struck without Serena being involved.

The two of them boarded a plane to Los Angeles where they had a meeting arranged with Milchan and his business partners. It was the kind of meeting that went on for hours … and hours. In fact, it lasted from around lunchtime until midnight. At one point, Serena was so tired she rested her head on the table and closed her eyes, but not before she got the answers she wanted to hear from the people offering to back her.

She wanted to know if they really believed in her so she asked them several questions, including whether she would receive a bonus if she won the US Open that year.

Milchan thought about it for a moment before replying: "OK, I'll give you a two-million-dollar bonus if you win the Open this year."

Serena smiled and nodded at the paper in front of him, making him write it down.

By the time they left Puma's offices, Serena had a sponsorship deal in place for the next five years with a brand that was promising to create a whole new line of tennis gear with her in mind. Most importantly to Serena though, was the fact that she felt Puma really believed in her. To them, she was more than just Venus's sister.

On the court, however, she was still struggling to shake off that label.

In her first appearance at a Grand Slam tournament, Serena was stopped in the second round by ... you guessed it, Venus. It was the 1998 Australian Open, a tournament that Serena entered ranked fifty-third in the world while Venus was sixteenth. From the moment the draw was made, the sisters prepared themselves for the possibility of a second-round clash between them – it would be their first match on one of the sport's biggest stages.

But first Serena had to get past her first-round match against the tournament's sixth seed, Irina Spirlea. Playing on centre court, she came back from losing the first set to record a major upset against her higher-ranked opponent and set up the tie that everyone – apart from those with the surname Williams – wanted to see.

After the match Serena joked,

# "WHAT'S LOVE GOT TO DO WITH IT?"

And when she spoke to the media about the prospect of beating Venus in the next round.

# "...WE BOTH WANT TO BE NUMBER ONE, AND I THINK IT DEPENDS ON WHICHEVER OF US IS MORE SERIOUS ABOUT IT."

The first set between the sisters was a tense, tight affair and Serena showed signs of feeling it. She served seven double faults and threw away a set point by hitting a forehand well wide of the sideline. Eventually, it was Venus who edged ahead, coming from behind to win the first-set tiebreak and take a one-set lead.

She didn't look back, racing ahead in the second set and winning it 6–1 to record her first victory over Serena on the professional stage. When the match was over, neither sister was smiling and when they met at the net for the usual handshake, Venus was quick to put her arm around Serena. She held on tight to her younger sister as they walked to the umpire's chair, where they joined hands and shared a bow in front of a cheering crowd.

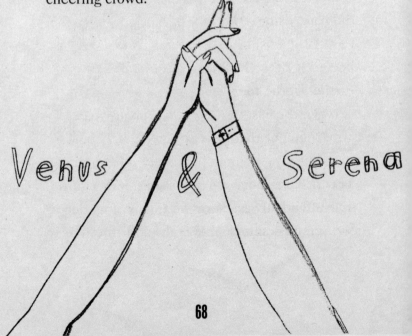

Venus & Serena

It had been a difficult match for their mum Oracene to watch (Richard didn't travel to the tournament). Sitting in the players' box she didn't quite know when to cheer or what to do. So, she mostly sat there with her fan and tried to keep her cool – in every sense of the word.

Afterwards Venus apologized for beating Serena and was quick to add that, "Serena hates to lose – her reputation is that she never loses to anyone twice."

Serena knew that Venus was the one everyone expected to win their match. She was playing well and had more experience. And even though Venus was right – she really did hate losing – there was a part of Serena that thought it was for the best that Venus did win, because she had a better chance of making it further in the tournament.

Nevertheless, the 1998 Australian Open was a tournament that Serena now sees as being a major turning point in her career. It announced her arrival and gave her something to aim for. Venus had always been the standard-bearer for Serena – someone she aimed to be like in every way – and now it finally felt like she was inching closer to her big sister.

One of the most notable things about seeing Venus and Serena on court together in Australia was how much Serena had closed the size gap on her sister. She had always been on the small size as a kid, but when Serena hit sixteen she had a growth spurt that had a huge impact on what she could do on the court. Suddenly she had the power to rival Venus and a serve that was well on the way to becoming a real weapon in the women's game.

The next month, Venus and Serena travelled to Oklahoma to play in a tournament called the IGA Tennis Classic, an indoor event played on hard courts. They were signed up to play in the singles and in the doubles together.

It proved to be a milestone week for them both. Venus defeated South Africa's Joannette Kruger to win the singles title – her first as a pro – beating the top seed Lindsay Davenport along the way. Then just thirty minutes after winning the final, she was back on court alongside Serena for the final of the women's doubles.

It was just the fifth time Venus and Serena had played together on the pro tour. They went into the tournament with a doubles ranking of 192nd in the world so it was some surprise when the sixteen- and seventeen-year-old sisters made it past the number one seeds in the quarter-finals and went on to reach the final.

Standing between them and the title was unseeded pair Catalina Cristea from Romania and Australian Kristine Kunce. They turned out to be no match for the Williams sisters who won the doubles title without dropping a set in the entire tournament. It meant Serena had won her first tour championship title alongside her best friend and that the two of them got to collect one of those giant cheques their dad had been so captivated by before they were born. This one was only for $4,500, but to Serena it felt just as good as winning a million dollars.

# GRAND SLAMS

There are four of these each year, with each one lasting for two weeks:

**Australian Open:** a hard-court tournament that takes place in Melbourne in January. It's held at the height of the Australian summer, so temperatures can soar as high as 40°C/104°F!

**French Open:** held on the dark red clay courts of Roland Garros in Paris in late May. The venue is named after famous French aviator and World War I fighter pilot Eugene Adrien Roland Georges Garros.

**Wimbledon:** the oldest tennis tournament in the world and the only grass court slam, which takes place in London, starting in late June. It's the only slam to enforce a strict all-white dress code.

**US Open:** the final slam of the year begins in late August and takes place in New York. It's played on hard courts at the Billie Jean King

National Tennis Centre where the main Arthur Ashe Stadium holds 23,771 people, making it the largest tennis stadium in the world.

By the end of 1998, Serena and Venus had collected another doubles title together and Serena had won her first Grand Slam titles, in the mixed doubles at Wimbledon and the US Open. On the singles court she was making steady progress too, reaching the fourth round of the French Open and the third round at Wimbledon and the US Open.

Ranked twentieth in the world at the beginning of 1999, few could have predicted that by the end of her second full year on the pro tour Serena would have won her first Grand Slam singles title.

It came at the fourth and final slam of the year, the US Open, where Venus had reached the final two years earlier. Earlier that year Serena had lost in the third round at the Australian Open and French Open and been forced to miss

Wimbledon with a back injury. But she had also won her first WTA Tour singles title, beating fellow teenager Amélie Mauresmo to win the Gaz de France tournament in March – on the same day that Venus won her fourth career singles title in Oklahoma.

## "THIS IS A START FOR ME,"

Serena said after that victory.

Winning her first singles title at seventeen years and five months meant Serena was three months younger than Venus had been when she'd won her first one. Finally, she had beaten Venus at something.

But the best was still to come.

Serena was seeded seventh going into the 1999 US Open (having climbed to a top ten ranking after winning tournaments in Indian Wells and Los Angeles) and eased through her first two rounds without dropping a set. But in the third round she faced an almighty tussle against fellow teenager Kim Clijsters and faced going out of the tournament when Clijsters was serving with a 5–3 lead in the third set.

Serena fought back hard though and won four games in a row to take the third set 7–5 and make it through to the second week of the tournament. She came from behind in her next two matches as well, losing the first set of her fourth-round match against Conchita Martinez and her first slam quarter-final against the number four seed Monica Seles. But she emerged victorious in both to set up an exciting semi-final against Lindsay Davenport.

Venus, meanwhile, was in the other semi-final, taking on Martina Hingis.

This time, Serena was the one to take the first set before Davenport hit back to win the second 6–1. The final set was a thrilling battle with both players exchanging powerful groundstrokes and landing booming serves. It was Serena who got the edge though, earning a crucial break of serve to take a lead she clung on to for the rest of the match.

There was no sign of nerves as she served for a place in her first Grand Slam final.

When Davenport hit a backhand return wide on match point, Serena threw her arms in the air and turned to face her dad in the crowd who could not hide his delight. The only sour note that day came when Venus lost her semi-final, meaning that the final would not be the all-Williams affair that Richard had predicted before the tournament. Instead, Serena was facing her sister's conqueror: world number one, Martina Hingis.

The two of them had already gone head-to-head once before in the tournament with Hingis using a press conference to respond to Richard Williams's claim that his daughters would be in the final. "They always have a big mouth. They always talk a lot," the eighteen-year-old told reporters. "But I like that, it's more pressure on them. Whether they can handle it or not now, that's the question."

Serena hit back in her own press conference shortly afterwards.

Before the final the two players called something of a truce. Hingis gave a signed T-shirt to Richard Williams and said that she and Serena had smoothed things over with a chat in the locker room.

But on the court, it was back to serious business as Hingis aimed to win her sixth Grand Slam title and Serena her first.

In the final moments before the match, Serena's dad reminded her that this was the moment they'd been working for all their lives. She just had to stay focused, take her chances and not be afraid.

If anyone looked afraid in the early stages it was not Serena, who raced into a 3–0 lead. Her aggressive, powerful groundstrokes proved too much for Hingis and although the world number one managed to break back at 2–4 down she then lost her serve again, allowing Serena to win the first set 6–3.

It was the American who got the first break once again in the second set and for a time it looked as though she was going to win her maiden slam in straightforward style. At 5–3 up, Serena had two championship points, but it was then that the realization of what she was about to achieve hit her.

As the nerves took hold, Serena's entire body tightened up. Suddenly her feet felt like they were made of stone and her accurate baseline strokes were replaced with wild shots that landed nowhere near the court. Before she knew it her two match points were gone and the momentum was firmly with her opponent.

Hingis was on top from then on and got the break of serve back to push the set into a tiebreak. The tension heightened as each player battled to inch ahead, with the crowd going wild after each and every point. Finally, with the scores level at 4–4 and Hingis serving, Serena went for it. After Hingis missed her first serve Serena took a big step into the court and pounced on her second serve, smashing a forehand return down the line. Hingis had no chance of reaching it.

Now, Serena had a 5–4 lead and two of her own serves to come. If she could win both those points, she would be the US Open champion.

The next point ended with two fierce backhands from Serena that forced Hingis into making an error. That made it 6–4: two more championship points for Serena.

This time she didn't let up. Another powerful backhand pushed the world number one into hitting a long return. The moment the ball landed, Serena's mouth dropped open in shock. Her screams of delight could be heard far and wide.

She could hardly believe it. It was so unexpected and yet it was something she had been preparing for since she was old enough to say the words: US Open.

After receiving the winners' cheque for $750,000 Serena spoke to the crowd, thanking her God Jehovah, her parents and sisters and the crowd for their support. As she lifted the trophy the television cameras panned across to her family where her dad was taking photographs and Venus was watching on, her face a mixture of pride and thoughts of "what might have been".

"It seems like for ever she's shared everything with her sister Venus," said the television commentators, "but now the stage belongs to Serena."

Even they were driving home the fact that despite all the attention being on Venus for so long, it was Serena who had become the first to win a Grand Slam title.

In doing so, she became the first Black woman

to win a Grand Slam title since Althea Gibson in 1958. And the fact that she won it on a court named after Arthur Ashe – the 1968 US Open champion and the last Black American to win a major – only made it more special. Serena later told the media,

## "IT'S REALLY AMAZING FOR ME TO EVEN HAVE AN OPPORTUNITY TO BE COMPARED TO A PLAYER AS GREAT AS ALTHEA GIBSON."

The 1999 US Open final was a match that Serena says changed her life and her career. She would never forget the moment when Hingis was serving at 4–4 in the tiebreak and she told herself she had to go for it. That if she didn't, she would regret it for the rest of her life. Even if she missed, it didn't matter. She just had to go for it.

It was this attitude that set the foundation for the rest of her career.

trophy

A few weeks after the US Open, the sisters experienced another big "first". Both reached the final of a tournament called the Grand Slam Cup in Munich, Germany, where only the best-performing players in the year's Grand Slams were invited to compete. It was their fourth meeting as professionals and so far, Venus had won them all.

But this time, all the momentum and confidence were with Serena. She dominated the early stages of the match, winning twelve of the first thirteen points and restricting Venus to just three points in the first five games. After winning the first set 6–1 Serena started making more mistakes and Venus was able to take advantage to level the score at one set all. But the US Open champ was not to be denied and broke her sister's serve to take a 3–1 lead in the third and final set, eventually winning it 6–3.

This time, Serena's reaction was not as joyous as it had been in New York. She held up her hand in recognition of the crowd's applause, but there was no jumping for joy or fist pumping. Venus was clapping her sister's performance from the other side of the net, and as the two met in the middle of the court they shared a hug.

Serena's win earned her $800,000 for winning the Grand Slam Cup title while she also got a $100,000 bonus for having won a Grand Slam that year. More importantly to her, she had extended her unbeaten run to sixteen matches, something she had only done once before (it was Venus who ended that run at a tournament in March that year).

By the end of the year, Serena was up to fourth in the world rankings, one place below Venus. But for all their delight at the way things were going on the court there were sad times away from it when Serena's parents Richard and Oracene told the family they were divorcing.

Serena had always considered her mum as the backbone of their family and her dad as the rest of the body. Together, they made up the whole and kept the Williams family in working order. Part of her worried what would happen now that they would no longer be together. How would the family function?

She and her sisters talked about it between themselves a lot. And they talked to their parents too, who reassured them that they would still love and be there for them all just the same as they always had been. The only difference was that they were no longer making each other happy, and that meant it was best for everybody if they moved on.

At first, it was strange and uncomfortable for them all. But little by little the Williams family adjusted to their new reality. Serena and Venus had plans to build a house of their own where they could live together and continue to support one another's journeys to the top of the game.

With the number one and two spots in the rankings now well within their sights it was no longer a matter of "if" one of them would make it but "when" and which one would do it first?

The following is the 1999 top ten ranked players in the world:

## WTA Singles Year-End Rankings

| Player | Points | Change | |
| --- | --- | --- | --- |
| Martina Hingis (SUI) | 6,074 | 1 | ▲ |
| Lindsay Davenport (USA) | 4,841 | 1 | ▼ |
| Venus Williams (USA) | 4,378 | 2 | ▲ |
| Serena Williams (USA) | 3,021 | 16 | ▲ |
| Mary Pierce (FRA) | 2,658 | 2 | ▲ |
| Monica Seles (USA) | 2,310 | | |
| Nathalie Tauziat (FRA) | 2,213 | 3 | ▲ |
| Barbara Schett (AUT) | 2,188 | 15 | ▲ |
| Julie Halard-Decugis (FRA) | 1,977 | 13 | ▲ |
| Amélie Mauresmo (FRA) | 1,906 | 19 | ▲ |

# TAKING A STAND

Growing up with four big sisters it was perhaps inevitable that Serena would develop an interest in fashion. As the youngest of the bunch it was often she who would get dressed up by Venus, Lyndrea, Isha and Tunde. When they wanted to try out new looks or hairstyles, they chose Serena as their mannequin.

When she was a young teenager, she started looking at fashion magazines and experimenting with different styles. She enjoyed figuring out what sort of things suited her and what didn't. Later on, her sponsorship deal with Puma gave her an opportunity to put some of that creativity into action. They were keen for Serena to work with them on the outfits they were designing for her to wear on the court. They wanted the look to be "as Serena" as possible and she was so excited about helping them to do that.

One of the standouts was a black catsuit that

she wore for the 2002 US Open. It was one of the most talked-about subjects of the tournament and led to almost as many questions in her first press conference as the match itself – mostly: is it comfortable?

Serena's catsuit

A couple of years before that outfit appeared, Serena had started college at the Art Institute of Fort Lauderdale.

Art institute of Fort Lauderdale

When she first finished high school, she hadn't thought about going to college at all. She thought she knew what she needed to know and what she didn't know, she could learn on her own.

There was just one problem with that: when she wasn't playing tennis, Serena was bored. There was only so much television she could watch (her favourite show was *The Golden Girls* and she'd already seen every episode twice), and Venus was keeping busy by signing up for a few courses at the Art Institute.

Eventually, Venus convinced Serena to do the same. She studied design and fashion which meant a lot of drawing, sewing and learning how different items of clothing were made.

The sisters weren't able to be full-time students because of their tennis careers. They could only complete one term each year, from the end of the tennis season in late autumn until the end of the year. So, a course that would normally take two-and-a-half years to complete took them a whole lot longer. But they stuck with it and, in the years that followed, used what they had learned to establish their own clothing ranges.

Venus launched her own brand called EleVen and Serena launched Aneres (her name spelled backwards), which later became known simply as Serena.

The first half of the year 2000 was largely a frustrating one for Serena. At the first slam of the year, she was seeded third, but was knocked out by sixteenth-seeded Russian, Elena Likhovtseva, in the fourth round. Her performance in that match was littered with mistakes – twenty unforced errors in the first set compared to Likhovtseva's six – leaving Serena determined to get back on the practice court the moment she got home from Australia.

She was back on the WTA Tour in February and March, but at a tournament in Amelia Island, Florida, in April she suffered a knee injury that kept her out of action until Wimbledon, meaning she was forced to sit out the second slam of the year, the French Open.

During that time, Serena added her voice and support to a protest that meant a lot to her. She had been signed up to play in a tournament called the Family Circle Cup in South Carolina, but decided not to play after finding out about a campaign started by the NAACP (the National Association for the Advancement of Coloured People). They were leading an economic boycott of South Carolina in protest at them flying the Confederate flag at the State House (the building housing the government of the state of South Carolina).

## THE CONFEDERATE FLAG

• The red, white and blue flag with thirteen stars, came into use during the American Civil War (1861–65). The war began when seven Southern states rebelled against the anti-slavery legislation proposed by President Abraham Lincoln and declared they were breaking away from the United States to form the Confederacy.

• The flag became known as a symbol of the American South and even after the

Confederate states were defeated it continued to be flown.

• During the civil rights movement in the 1950s and 1960s the flag became a symbol of segregation and was adopted by the Ku Klux Klan (an American hate group that sees white people as superior to all other races and whose primary target is African-Americans).

• Supporters of the flag say it honours Southern heritage which is different to the cultural traditions of the rest of the United States.

• Opponents of the flag say it is a symbol of racism, hatred and slavery.

Serena said that her decision not to play in South Carolina was based on an issue that she felt very strongly about. By pulling out of the tournament, she was making sure that as many people as possible were aware of the issue and adding pressure to the state lawmakers to remove a flag that many felt should not be on display at an official government building. Eventually her stand, allied to that of many others, resulted in the flag being moved elsewhere.

It would not be the last time Serena stood up for something she believed strongly in.

She returned to the WTA Tour in time for Wimbledon and, despite having been out of action since April, was seeded eighth for the tournament. Even that started to look a little low though as she cruised through the opening rounds without losing a set, dropping just a few games in each match.

Every round she breezed through was taking her a step closer to a semi-final against Venus – a match that would be their fifth meeting as professionals and the first one to take place on grass.

Neither Richard nor Oracene was in the Centre Court crowd to watch this one. Oracene was back in Florida, preferring to watch her daughters go head-to-head from the privacy of her own home. Richard was at Wimbledon, but spent the match walking around the grounds of the All England Club, too nervous to sit and watch the match from start to finish.

Serena entered the semi-final as most people's favourite to win. Her form throughout the tournament had been so good that it seemed no one could touch her – not even her big sister.

But Venus had something that Serena no longer did: the desire to win her very first Grand Slam. On this occasion, it gave her the extra bit of focus she needed to get the better of Serena in front of a crowd that was captivated by the emotion and tension of such an important match taking place between two sisters.

Two sisters who had shared a room the night before their match, just as they always had done.

As they both relaxed into the match, it became clear just how well they knew each other's games. Shots that would take any other player by surprise by their power or ferocity were returned with relative ease. Even Serena's booming serve – which often left her opponents scrambling simply to get a racquet on to the ball – was coming back with extra oomph from Venus.

The first set was going to serve until the fourth game when Venus capitalized on some unusual double faults from Serena to take the lead. She broke back in the next game, but then lost her serve again, from which point Venus pressed home her advantage to win the first set 6–2.

When Serena took a 4–2 lead in the second set, it looked as though the match might go to a third set. But then something changed. She lost all consistency on her forehand and began to struggle to return Venus's serve. Before she knew it, Venus had won three straight games and was now leading 5–4!

The match moved into a tiebreak to see whether Venus was going to win in straight sets or if Serena could force it into a deciding third set.

It was the older sister who was able to keep her composure the better. She edged ahead by four points to three and took the next two to earn a match point on Serena's serve.

That was the moment Serena's trusty weapon deserted her. She served her sixth double fault of the day to hand Venus the victory and a place in her first Wimbledon final.

Venus didn't celebrate. She didn't even smile. Instead, she looked sad that she had knocked her little sister out of the competition. When they met at the net Venus saw the tears gathering in Serena's eyes. She placed a protective arm around her shoulder and whispered in her ear, "Let's get out of here."

## DID YOU KNOW?

........................................................

**Venus Williams holds the record for the fastest serve ever recorded by a female player at Wimbledon. In 2008 she hit a 129 mph serve. The men's record is 148 mph and was recorded by another American, Taylor Dent, in 2010.**

........................................................

Two days later, Venus was back on Centre Court for the final, this time facing the defending Wimbledon champion, Lindsay Davenport. With everyone wondering when she was going to match her younger sister in winning a Grand Slam, Venus was under pressure to win.

When she finally managed it, beating Davenport

6–3, 7–6, Venus allowed herself to celebrate at last. She danced across the court and ran up the stairs that led to the box where Serena and her dad were sitting, wrapping her arms around her little sister who was grinning from ear to ear.

Venus had become the first African-American woman to win Wimbledon since Althea Gibson in 1958, and in the aftermath of her victory Davenport predicted that both sisters would go on to win many more slams.

She was right. In fact, Venus went on to win another one just a few months later at the US Open, beating Davenport again in the final. It gave the Williams family some revenge after Davenport had knocked Serena out of the competition at the quarter-final stage – the first time in five meetings that Serena had lost to Davenport.

The slams might not have brought much joy for Serena that year, but soon after the US Open, she was given the chance to travel to Australia as part of the US Olympic team for the 2000 Games taking place in Sydney. The singles players were selected on their ranking so Venus, Lindsay

Davenport and Monica Seles were picked to play in the singles tournament. But Serena was selected to play in the doubles with Venus.

Together, they had won all three of the Grand Slam doubles finals they'd reached and were so excited about getting the chance to compete on behalf of their country. It's not something that tennis players actually get to do very often, so when the Olympics come around once every four years, it's an event they all look forward to.

Venus continued her winning ways in Sydney. In the women's singles final, she defeated Russia's Elena Dementieva to win the gold medal. One day later, she was back on court for the final of the women's doubles with Serena. It took the sisters just fifty minutes to defeat their Dutch opponents, Kristie Boogert and Miriam Oremans, 6-1, 6-1, and earn another gold medal for the USA.

Venus later said that winning gold with her sister and best friend was almost a better feeling than winning gold in the singles had been.

For Serena, the moment was one to savour, too:

# "EVERY YEAR I CAN WIN A SLAM. THIS IS EVERY FOUR YEARS, AND YOU NEVER KNOW WHAT'S GOING TO HAPPEN."

## WHAT IS THE FED CUP?

- The Fed Cup takes place every season and is an international team competition for female tennis players (the men's equivalent is called the Davis Cup).

- Aside from the Olympics, it's the only tournament where players compete on behalf of their country.

- In 2020, a total of 116 nations entered the

Fed Cup making it the world's largest annual international team competition in women's sport.

• The USA won the first ever Fed Cup held in 1963 and have the best record of any nation in the competition. They've reached thirty finals and won eighteen of them. Great Britain have reached four finals and so far, have won none.

Following the Olympics, Venus and Serena made the decision to cut back on their tennis schedule a little so that they could concentrate on their studies. Some people took that as a sign that their interest in the sport was fickle – that they might not be in it for the long haul.

But Venus and Serena believed that having outside interests was the best way to ensure they would stay in the sport for a long time. It gave them room to breathe; time to refresh themselves mentally and physically. Besides, who wants to fill their life with just one thing? It would be like only ever eating one flavour of ice cream, and that's just dull.

Inspired by her older sister's successful year, Serena started 2001 determined to add to the sole Grand Slam title she'd won in New York two years earlier. At the first slam of the year in Australia she made it to the quarter-finals without dropping a set. But then she came up against Martina Hingis – a player who on that day was able to match Serena's levels of determination and grit.

The match was a thriller from start to finish. After Hingis won the first set 6–2 Serena came back to win the second 6–3 and used that momentum to take a 4–1 lead in the deciding third set. But Hingis refused to be beaten and clawed her way back into the match, levelling the set at 4–4.

Every point was a war of wills between the two. Some rallies went on for so long that people in the crowd got neck ache from turning their heads from one side of the court to the other so many times.

At that time, there were no tiebreaks used in the final set of Grand Slam matches. So once the score reached 6–6 in the final set (the third set for women and fifth set for men), play would simply continue until one player won two games in a row. That meant matches could theoretically continue for hours, or even days.

## LONGEST MATCHES

• The longest ever women's singles match took place on 24 September 1984 between Vicki Nelson and Jean Hepner, the number 93 and number 172 ranked players in the world. It lasted for six hours and thirty-one minutes and also featured the longest point ever played in a professional tennis match: a 643-shot rally that lasted twenty-nine minutes. Eventually Nelson won the match 6–4, 7–6 (13–11 in the tiebreak).

• The longest ever men's singles match was between Nicolas Mahut and John Isner at Wimbledon in 2010. Lasting eleven hours and five minutes and spread over the course of three days (thanks to two stoppages for darkness), the epic finished 6–4, 3–6, 6–7, (7–9), 7–6, (7–3), 70–68 – with Isner emerging as the exhausted winner.

In this case, the end came relatively swiftly. Hingis won her service game to take a 7–6 lead and then earned two match points against Serena's serve. Serena saved the first one with a brave and brilliant drop shot, but she could not repeat the feat, leaving Hingis to progress to a semi-final meeting with Venus (whom she ended up beating 6–1, 6–1). She lost the final to Jennifer Capriati, but had achieved the rare feat of beating both Williams sisters in the same tournament.

The next part of the season was usually a favourite of Serena's. She got to play in back-to-back tournaments on a surface she loved (hard courts), and in places where she felt at home: Indian Wells, California and Miami, Florida.

In 2001, Serena headed to the first of those tournaments in Indian Wells with high hopes. Two years earlier she had beaten the legendary German player Steffi Graf in the Indian Wells final to win her biggest title up to that point. From then on it had been one of her favourite tournaments. Not only because it held memories of that victory, but because it was one of the few tournaments where the Williams family could all be together. Indian Wells was close to where Yetunde (Serena's oldest sister) lived in Los Angeles, which meant she could spend a few days there with them. It was something that Serena looked forward to for months.

The draw placed Serena into the same half as Venus meaning that if they made it that far, the sisters would face off in the semi-finals. Serena had only won one of their five meetings as professionals, but she felt she was playing well and was ready for another shot at beating her big sister.

Everything went to plan. In their respective quarter-finals, Venus lost just three games en route to beating Russian Elena Dementieva and Serena matched that by easing past Lindsay Davenport 6–1, 6–2. Everything looked set for a huge semi-final battle between them.

But it didn't pan out that way. Despite the

scoreline making it look easy, Venus had started to feel pain in her knee during the match against Dementieva. She worried that it might affect her ability to play in the semi-finals, but decided to sleep on it and see if it felt better on the morning of the match.

Sadly, it did not. Venus travelled with Serena to the stadium as usual and looked for the WTA Tour trainer to tell him that she didn't think she was able to play. But the trainer and tournament director wanted to give her as much time as possible to see if she might change her mind. No one wanted to see Venus pull out and take away the possibility of a great match between her and Serena.

It got to the point where Serena had done her warm-up and the fans were inside the stadium, waiting patiently for the entrance of Venus and Serena. Finally, with five minutes to go before the match was scheduled to begin, a tournament spokesperson made the announcement that Venus was withdrawing due to injury.

The crowd went crazy. They were upset at the lateness of the decision and couldn't understand why Venus's decision wasn't made earlier. Even the tournament director Charlie Pasarell was later heard to say: "I only wish she had at least gone out and given it a try. This hurts the game of tennis more than the individual tournament."

Ridiculous rumours started circulating that Richard had told Venus to pull out so that Serena could make it through to the final – false allegations that Serena later said, "hurt, cut and ripped into us deeply."

It all seemed so unfair. Venus had made it clear from the moment she arrived at the stadium that she wouldn't be able to play that day and yet she felt she was being blamed for the lateness of the message being passed on to the crowd.

Serena did what she could to ignore the noise and focus on the final taking place two days later. She was up against a young Belgian player named Kim Clijsters who had beaten the world number one, Martina Hingis, in the semi-finals and – at just seventeen years old – was two years younger than Serena. But Serena had won their two previous meetings and felt confident that she could make it three out of three on a court she considered her "home turf".

From the moment she walked on to the court though, it was obvious that the crowd no longer considered her their favourite.

There were loud boos coming from what felt like all corners of the stadium. Serena didn't know what to do. She'd never experienced anything like it before. It felt even worse when Clijsters walked on to the court to be greeted by a chorus of cheers.

What had she done wrong? Serena couldn't figure it out. She would later write that in a game she loved, at one of her most cherished tournaments, she suddenly felt unwelcome, alone and afraid.

She wanted to cry, but at the same time she didn't want to give those people booing her the satisfaction of knowing they had got to her.

As Serena and Clijsters finished their warm-up, Venus and Richard Williams entered the stadium and started walking down the steps to their seats in the players' box. At that moment Serena became aware of a subtle change in the crowd noise: it was no longer directed at her, but at her family.

Then she realized. The crowd were booing because of the cancelled semi-final match between her and Venus. As she looked up into the crowd, she could see people shouting and pointing towards her sister and dad. How was she supposed to concentrate on playing a match when her family was being treated like that?

Serena did her best to refocus on the match. As it got under way it became clear that the crowd were going to continue to make their feelings clear. Clijsters held her serve easily in the first game to great applause. And when Serena missed the first serve of her opening service game, they were equally overjoyed.

## WAS IT RACISM?

• A commentator on the match said: "An American crowd booing an American family ... and you have to say that it does smack of a little bit of racism."

- Serena later said she believed that too. Her father heard people shouting racial slurs and cries of, "Go back to Compton." She later wrote in *Time* magazine that "the undercurrent of racism was painful, confusing and unfair".

- Serena was not claiming that everyone in the crowd that day was racist, but that there were racist elements to it. And sadly, even when it is a minority of people saying or doing the wrong thing, it is those people who seem to make the most noise.

As Serena tried to block out what was going on, Clijsters won the opening seven points of the first set. Serena started to fear she might never find her way into the match.

The first set went the way of her Belgian opponent, but neither of them were playing particularly well. Both were making more mistakes than they usually would, and Serena was struggling to see how she was going to come out on top.

At 2–1 down in the second set, she sat on her chair at the changeover, buried her head in her towel and cried.

It was the lowest Serena had felt on a tennis court. But then her mind drifted to Althea Gibson and to all the things she had overcome during her time as a tennis player. If Althea could battle through all of that then, Serena told herself, she could come through this. She thought about her dad too and everything he had endured growing up in Shreveport.

He was the reason that she and Venus had been able to overcome all the odds to make it this far – to a position where they were showing other young, Black athletes that they were capable of achieving whatever they put their minds to.

Suddenly, she saw the match in a new light: it wasn't just her against Clijsters, it was her against Clijsters and those people in the crowd who were booing her every move.

Before the changeover was over, Serena said a prayer. She wasn't praying to win, but for the strength to persevere; to get up from her chair and finish the match.

She couldn't let those people win. She refused to let them win.

The next two sets were error strewn from both players. It was as though neither of them could maintain their concentration for long enough to really dominate the match. But Serena managed to win the second set 6–4, momentarily quieting the crowd. Clijsters won the first game of the deciding set, but then the momentum swung dramatically in Serena's favour and she raced to a 5–1 lead.

Soon afterwards she was serving for the match in front of a crowd that had booed her from start to finish. As her crosscourt forehand landed with too much power for Clijsters to return, Serena raised her arms in triumph and waved to the crowd, as she always did after a victory.

Indian Wells Open

The boos came back loud and clear. They were accompanied by a few cheers, but nowhere near enough to drown out the negative response to Serena's win.

After collecting her trophy and cheque for $330,000 on the court, Serena was handed the microphone for the usual winners' speech. She took a deep breath, forced a smile and said:

# "I'D LIKE TO THANK EVERYONE WHO SUPPORTED ME, AND IF YOU DIDN'T, I LOVE YOU GUYS ANYWAY."

As she left the court, she could not stop the tears from rolling down her face. She was proud of herself for making it through, but mostly all she felt was sadness. She might have won the tournament, but she felt as if she had actually lost something far more important – the fight for equality. The experience impacted on her and Venus so badly that they both decided they would not return to the tournament. Serena wanted to make a stand, just as she had over the issue of the Confederate flag. She was scared of walking out on to the court at Indian Wells and receiving the same response – it was something she never wanted to go through again. It was the only way she could make sure that no one forgot about what happened that day, and that no other athlete would ever have to go through the same thing that she did in Indian Wells.

# SERENA SLAM

**R**ichard Williams was left in no doubt that the courage shown by his youngest daughter at Indian Wells was that of a true champion.

On the very biggest stages, Serena was struggling to produce the tennis to match that courage. At both the French Open and Wimbledon in the summer of 2001, she was knocked out in the quarter-finals, leaving Venus to add a second Wimbledon title to her growing list. As a result, arriving at the US Open that year all eyes were once again on Venus and whether she could repeat the Wimbledon/US Open double of the previous year.

Serena had won her second event of the year the week before the US Open, beating Jennifer Capriati to win the Rogers Cup in Toronto. After a few knee problems and a stomach virus had troubled her at previous tournaments, she finally felt fit and healthy. And in the days before the

US Open started, she left reporters in no doubt about her aims in New York: "It's been a long time since I've done anything," she said. "I would like to do something here. And I'm really looking forward to making it happen."

There was just one problem: the draw.

If Serena was to win the US Open that year, she was going to have to overcome a tough route to the final. It would probably include the sixth seed, Justine Henin, third seed, Lindsay Davenport and the top seed, Martina Hingis. If she could beat all of them then her opponent for the title would most likely be Venus.

One by one, Serena faced them all. Henin was beaten in straight sets. Davenport in three. And then in the semi-finals she recorded a fifty-three-minute long, straight sets win over Hingis that left no one in any doubt about how much Serena wanted to win her second US Open title.

From the moment Venus won match point in her semi-final against Capriati, the build up to the Williams sisters' face-off started. It was a historic occasion for the sport: two American players, sisters, meeting in a Grand Slam final.

Not only was it the first time that two sisters had contested the final of a slam since Maud and Lilian Watson in 1884, but it was the first time ever that two African-American players had ever met in a final.

It was such a big deal that the tournament organizers decided that instead of the women's final taking place on a Saturday afternoon as it usually did, this one should take place on Saturday night in prime time.

## MAUD AND LILIAN WATSON

• Maud Edith Eleanor Watson was the first ever winner of a ladies' singles title at Wimbledon. In 1884, three years after she started playing competitive tennis, she beat her sister, Lilian, 6–8, 6–3, 6–3 in the final to win the title and was awarded a silver flower basket valued at twenty Guineas. Lilian walked away with a silver-backed hairbrush worth ten Guineas.

A 100-strong gospel choir got the night under way before Diana Ross sang "God Bless America". The crowd was even treated to an impressive fireworks display. It was quite the build-up for a tennis match.

For the opening four games, the match went with serve and the crowd watched on, hopeful that an epic was about to unfold. But Venus had other ideas. After breaking her sister's serve in the fifth game, she pressed her foot down on the accelerator and did not look back, wrapping up the set 6–2.

She broke Serena's serve in the opening game of the second set too, but the younger sister was not beaten yet and fought her way back into the match, much to the delight of the crowd who were desperate to see a third set.

It was not to be, as Venus's consistency trumped the more wayward power of her sister's play. Venus wrapped up the second set and the match 6–4, courtesy of another unforced error from Serena. Once again, she did not celebrate her victory, but instead met Serena at the net, told her she loved her and wrapped her long arms around her little sister before sitting down with her at the side of the court.

# "I'M DISAPPOINTED, BUT ONLY A LITTLE, BECAUSE VENUS WON,"

Serena said after the match. Losing to Venus was always hard, but she could still take some pleasure from the fact it was her sister who would be lifting the trophy. And she was still only nineteen years old. Other chances would come her way. In the meantime, she just had to learn as much as possible from every final she played in so that when the time did come, she would be able to take them.

Serena had to wait longer than she wanted for the next chance to come around. At the beginning of the next season she was playing at a warm-up event for the Australian Open when she twisted her ankle in the middle of a match.

She retired from the match and hoped that after a few days' rest she would be fit enough to play in the first slam of 2002. But in her final practice session before the tournament began her ankle was still affecting her movement and so she had no choice but to pull out.

By the time Serena returned to the WTA Tour in late February, Venus had placed her name firmly into the history books. After winning two tournaments early in the year (and reaching the quarter-finals of the Australian Open) she had leapfrogged Jennifer Capriati to become the new world number one. Venus was the first African-American woman of the Open Era ever to hold the top spot, and the second of all time after Althea Gibson.

Serena was excited for her sister, but eager to return to court so that she could start climbing up those rankings too. Her first tournament back gave her the best possible start as she had a great run to the final of a WTA event in Scottsdale, Arizona, and went on to beat Capriati in the final.

It gave Serena her first tournament win of the year and set her on a path that would take the tennis world by storm.

A month after her win in Scottsdale, Serena won her second title of the year at the Miami Open, beating the three top-ranked players in the world to do so: Hingis, Venus and Capriati (who by then had taken back the number one spot from Venus).

But winning the title wasn't the most memorable moment of the week for Serena. That came in the semi-final when she recorded her first win over Venus since 1999. Serena was in shock. To her Venus was the best player out there and to beat her felt like a huge milestone.

She had already won one Grand Slam of course, but Serena felt that had come so early in her career that she was still developing her game. Now she felt truly ready to challenge for the biggest titles in the sport.

The next slam on the calendar was the French Open – the only one of the four to take place on a clay court. Serena's best run in Paris had come the previous year when she reached the quarter-finals, but it had never been a surface she was particularly consistent on – not like the hard courts she had grown up playing on.

# PLAYING ON CLAY

- Clay courts are not actually made of clay. Each court is around three feet deep and consists of four layers of different stones. On top of the base sits a thick layer of white powdered limestone and three millimetres of fine red sand (which gives the French Open courts that dark red colour).

- The red material makes the ball more visible and the surface more slippery, enabling players to slide as they move around the court.

- Clay courts play slower than hard or grass courts making rallies longer and meaning it is much harder to hit a winning shot.

- The white lines of a clay court are usually made of plastic so if the ball hits one players have to be prepared for it to shoot through really fast.

- The courts can also play slightly differently depending on the weather. On a warm, dry day they will play a little faster and the ball will bounce higher. On a cloudy, wet day the same court will play slower and the ball bounce lower.

clay tennis court

Leading up to the tournament Serena competed in warm-up events in Berlin and Rome and reached the final in both, each time facing the same opponent: Justine Henin. She lost to the Belgian in the first one, but got her revenge in Rome. Serena now had her first ever title on clay and headed to Paris confident that she was a real threat for the French Open title.

Justine Henin

She was seeded third, behind Venus and Capriati, and all three reached the semi-final stage without too much bother. There, Serena was up against Capriati while Venus took on unseeded Argentine Clarisa Fernandez for a place in the final.

As expected, Serena's task proved the tougher of the two. Capriati took the first set and despite being 5–2 down in the second clawed her way back to force a tiebreak. At that point, all the momentum was on Capriati's side. Serena had to dig as deep as she possibly could to make sure she won the tiebreak and stayed in the match.

She did just that and in the third set Capriati crumbled while Serena only got stronger, winning it 6–2.

## "I NEVER THINK OF LOSING,"

she said after the match, explaining that negative thoughts only hindered her.

With Venus also winning her semi-final, the sisters were going head-to-head in another Grand Slam final – although it was the first time either of them had reached that stage of the French Open. The best bit was that no matter which of them won, they knew that when the

WTA rankings were updated the following week, they would make history as the first sisters to be ranked number one (Venus) and two (Serena) in the world.

Richard Williams's dream was coming true.

## DID YOU KNOW?

........................................................

**By reaching the final, Venus passed ten million dollars in career prize money.**

........................................................

Serena was desperate to win another slam, and with her victory over Venus in Miami fresh in her memory she went into the final in Paris in confident mood. There she found a Venus who was far from her best, struggling with her serve and hitting groundstrokes that lacked their usual punch.

For a crowd who hoped for a classic, the error-strewn match might have disappointed. But taking each other on in a Grand Slam final was something that neither could really get used to. They both found it uncomfortable. And on this occasion it seemed to affect Venus in particular, her nine double faults handing Serena more gifts than she would have expected.

The match ended 7–5, 6–3 to Serena. On winning match point she threw her arms in the air and dropped her racquet to the ground before leaning forward and resting her hands on her knees. It was her moment to try and soak everything in. Three years after winning the US Open she had finally won her second Grand Slam, proven she was not a "one-hit wonder" and beaten Venus. It was almost too much to take in.

When she met Venus at the net the hug from her big sister was as warm as ever. Later, as Serena collected the winner's trophy, she spotted a familiar face among the throng of photographers. Venus had grabbed her mum's camera and found the perfect spot to take a picture for the family album.

Venus and Serena were now undoubtedly the biggest names in the sport and the rest of the year only proved it. The Wimbledon and US Open finals were both all-Williams affairs with

Serena coming out on top on each occasion. Their dad had always said that one day they would be playing in the finals of the biggest tournaments in the world and now a decade later, that's exactly what they were doing.

It was the kind of dominance that attracted some bitterness from others within the game, but Serena didn't care. "People are never satisfied and that's just the truth," she said after her US Open triumph. "You have to be satisfied with you and who you are. Venus and I have learned that we're satisfied and we're happy with us."

Serena had won three of the year's four Grand Slams, each on different surfaces and ended 2002 as the world number one. It was a year that secured her status as a true superstar of the sport.

## SERENA'S 2002 IN NUMBERS

**56** WINS: **5** DEFEATS

**8** SINGLES TITLES WON

**32** CONSECUTIVE SETS WON IN GRAND SLAMS

**4** MATCHES PLAYED AGAINST VENUS:

**4** VICTORIES

Venus knew what she was talking about. At the Australian Open in January 2003 the sisters went head-to-head for a fourth consecutive Grand Slam final. It was the first one to go to three sets, with Serena winning the first and Venus the second. But it was the world number one who came out on top, completing her hold on all four Grand Slam titles.

When a player can tick off winning all four Grand Slams it is called a "career Grand Slam". Serena had not only done that, but held all four at the same time. It was something only four other women had ever done and considered very special. So special that people started to call it the "Serena Slam".

Serena seemed unstoppable.

But at the French Open, back where her run started a year earlier, Serena's incredible series of grand-slam victories came to a bit of a bad-tempered end.

She reached the semi-finals smoothly enough, but then came up against Justine Henin-Hardenne (her married name at the time). The Belgian had already inflicted one defeat on Serena that year, ending her 21–0 start to the 2003 season by beating her in the final of the Family Circle Cup tournament in Charleston, USA in April. "Today we could see she could be frustrated," Henin-Hardenne said after her win. "I think it's good for the other players that we can see that."

When the two met again in the semi-final of the French Open the following month Serena was more motivated than ever. "I'm on a mission," she said after breezing through her quarter-final win over Amelie Mauresmo in barely an hour. But her opponent was no less determined and came out strongly in the first set, breaking Serena in her first two service games and eventually winning it 6–2. Serena fought back to win the second 6–4 and take the match into a deciding third set, which is where her problems really started.

The French Open traditionally attracts a lot of Belgian fans and as they not only had Henin-Hardenne, but also Kim Clijsters in the latter stages of the tournament, there were perhaps an even larger number than usual there for the match. For most of the match they had been more pro-Henin-Hardenne than anti-Serena, but midway through the third set, that changed.

It started when Henin-Hardenne hit a groundstroke that landed close to the baseline. Before the line judge could make their call, Serena stopped playing and circled the mark where the ball had bounced – it was wide of the line. Serena was right, but the crowd was upset with the way she had pointed it out and started to boo and jeer.

Before the noise could subside Serena went to serve, not seeing until the last minute that Henin-Hardenne had raised her hand to show she was not ready. When Serena's serve landed out, she told the umpire she had been distracted, but he hadn't seen the Belgian's gesture and Henin-Hardenne stayed quiet. Serena was left with no choice but to go ahead with a second serve, but was clearly unsettled and didn't win another point in the game.

Every shot she missed was greeted with loud cheers from a crowd that now seemed not only to have sided with Henin-Hardenne, but to have turned against Serena. The Belgian went on to close out the set 7–5 ending Serena's run of thirty-one unbeaten Grand Slam matches and leaving her to walk off court to a loud chorus of boos.

In the post-match press conference, Serena couldn't stop the tears from falling.

Serena did not have to wait long to meet Henin-Hardenne again. A few weeks after their match in Paris, they were on opposite sides of the net in a Wimbledon semi-final. This time, though, Serena gave her opponent barely a sniff of victory, striking the ball with such ferocity that at one point a policeman behind the baseline had to take evasive action to prevent his helmet being blasted off his head by the tail end of a Serena smash.

After a 6–3, 6–2 victory that set up a sixth Grand Slam final against Venus, Serena played down any talk of a rivalry between herself and Henin-Hardenne, describing the Belgian as "a nice girl", and a "good player". All she wanted was to get back to winning ways, so the victory was sweet no matter who it came against.

While playing Venus for a title was nothing new to Serena, playing an injured Venus was. Her big sister aggravated an abdominal injury during her semi-final against Kim Clijsters and played through pain to win it. Now Serena had to try and override her sisterly instincts telling her to take it easy on Venus and focus on defending her Wimbledon title.

In the opening set it looked as though it was Serena who was most bothered by the taping on Venus's stomach and upper left leg. Within the blink of an eye Serena was 3–0 down in the first set and missing more shots than she was making. But when Venus started to miss her first serves Serena was able to break back and work her way into the match, levelling the set at 3–3 before her own errors helped Venus clinch the opening set 6–4.

The second set started with three straight breaks of serve, but this time it was Serena who took control, establishing a 5–1 lead.

Venus cut it to 5–4, but Serena held her nerve to win the next game and level up at one set all.

It was only then that Venus's injury problems started to become more apparent. Her opening service game was filled with errors and after hitting her final serve she winced in pain, her hand moving instinctively to the left side of her stomach. She took an injury timeout, leaving the court briefly to have the taping on her stomach reapplied, but from then on her serves lacked their usual power.

"I just had to tell myself to look at the ball and nothing else," Serena later said about her ability to shut out her concern for her sister and win the third set 6–2. She paid tribute to her Venus's bravery too, saying: "I knew she was tough, but she's gone on to a whole different level. To play today knowing she was injured, she's definitely up there with the real fighters and champions."

Serena's second Wimbledon title was her sixth Grand Slam overall and she was still just twenty-one years old. At that moment it looked as though the sky was the limit on what she could achieve. But over the next twelve

months or so she would face some of her most
challenging times yet – on or off the court.

## INJURY TIMEOUTS IN TENNIS

• If a player is struggling with injury
or illness during a match they can ask
the umpire to call the physiotherapist or
tournament doctor, who then assesses the
player during the next changeover or set
break (unless it's an acute condition that
needs immediate medical treatment).

• If the physio decides that treatment is
needed they can request a Medical Time Out,
which means they get a maximum of three
minutes to treat the player. This treatment
can take place off the court if needed for
privacy reasons.

• Players are only allowed one Medical
Time Out per condition during a single

match. If they need further treatment for the same problem it has to take place within the regular changeover time and they can only have it on two more occasions.

# FAMILY TIES

**S**erena loves to dance. Sometimes, too much.

Not long after picking up her second Wimbledon title she was on a night out in Los Angeles, doing what she loved to do on the dance floor. But one lapse of concentration and an ambitious spin move later she felt something in her knee that she immediately knew was bad news.

Her left thigh muscle had partially detached from her knee and to repair it she needed surgery. She felt terrible. Her parents had put so much time and effort into giving her the foundations to build a career and now she felt like she had let them down. Initially it was announced that Serena would be out of action for a couple of months, but it ended up being a whole lot longer than that.

Serena based herself in Los Angeles while she was recovering from her surgery. It meant she was closer to her eldest sister Tunde (Yetunde) and in the right place to pursue one of her other big passions while she was unable to compete: acting. For a while Tunde worked as Serena's personal assistant, helping to arrange her busy schedule and keep on top of the many emails and calls she got every day. During that time she felt closer to Tunde than she had since the family had moved away to Florida leaving Tunde behind in California. They spoke on the phone every single day.

In September 2003 Serena was in Toronto, Canada, filming a television advert when she received a phone call she would never forget. It was from her mum, telling her she was worried about Tunde. She'd gone out and Oracene couldn't get hold of her on the phone. Serena told her not to worry, that it wasn't so late out and she was sure Tunde was fine.

But something in her mum's voice made Serena worry, so she picked up the phone and called Tunde's house. That's when she heard the news. Tunde had been involved in an accident – a shooting – and she hadn't survived.

It was devastating for the Williams family.

Over the painful weeks and months that followed they did the only thing they could to get through it: they leaned on each other.

Neither Venus or Serena played again that year although both were also still recovering from injuries – Serena with her knee and Venus with the abdominal injury that had affected her Wimbledon campaign. As January rolled into view, Venus got back into her stride. She competed in the Australian Open, but suffered her earliest exit ever from the first slam of the season, losing in the third round. "I'm pretty much in shock," she said afterwards.

Serena wasn't yet ready, emotionally or physically, to return to the tour. It was late March by the time she felt that her knee was in good enough shape for her to compete again – eight months after she'd walked off Wimbledon's Centre Court with the winner's trophy.

She thought it would be good for her to have tennis to focus on again. Without it she felt like she was just going through the motions; not only of rehab, but of grieving for her sister.

Serena's first tournament back was at the Miami Open where nobody quite knew what to expect from her after such a lengthy absence. But she eased through to the final, dropping just one set along the way. Once there, she crushed her opponent Elena Dementieva 6–1, 6–1 to win her third Miami Open title. It was the perfect response to those who had questioned her passion for the sport in the time she had been away.

The year would end without a Grand Slam win for Serena though – the first time she had finished a season without winning one since 2001. At the French Open she was beaten in the quarter-finals and at Wimbledon she reached the final, but was beaten by a relative newcomer to the Tour, Maria Sharapova.

At the US Open, she once again reached the quarter-finals before losing to Jennifer Capriati in a match that would end up being remembered for lots of reasons – not all of them good.

First, the good: Serena's outfit. Some players don't place any importance on what they wear on the court; they see it as irrelevant to how they play. But for Serena, looking her best on court was tied to how she felt when she was out there. When there was an edge to how she looked there was an edge to her game. She loved the fact that she was developing her own trademark style on court – it gave her a sense of power that transferred into her tennis.

By the time she played in the 2004 US Open, she had signed a new sponsorship contract with Nike (worth an estimated forty million dollars over five years). Together they came up with an outfit for the tournament that would be a first in the women's game: denim.

In Serena's first match of the tournament people couldn't believe what they were seeing: a denim skirt! For tennis! The material was actually a "sport denim", meaning there was some give to it when she was darting around the court. It was paired with a studded black tank top and black boots that unzipped to reveal black trainers once the warm-up was done and it was time to get serious. She called it

denim skirt

her "signature look" and she loved that it made an impression.

When it came to the tennis she was turning heads too, making it through to the quarter-finals with relative ease. Then she ran into Capriati in a match that is considered one of the catalysts for the "challenge system" that was adopted soon afterwards.

## HOW DOES HAWK-EYE WORK?

- Hawk-eye is the name of a line-calling system that traces a ball's trajectory and sends it to a virtual-reality machine.

- It uses six or more computer-linked television cameras situated around the tennis court.

• A centralized computer system rapidly processes the images from these cameras, maps the position of the ball and calculates a flight path – the yellow streak you see behind the ball in the Hawk-eye graphics.

# THE CHALLENGE SYSTEM

• If a player feels a wrong call has been made by a line judge or umpire they can "challenge" it and Hawk-eye will show the exact point where the ball landed.

• Each player is allowed a maximum of three unsuccessful challenges per set, with an additional one if the set reaches a tiebreak.

• Most clay court tournaments (including the French Open) don't use Hawk-eye because it's felt that the marks left in the sand offer evidence enough of where a ball lands.

So, what happened? There were hints in the very first set of what was to come when Serena hit a baseline winner that was called long. She questioned the call, but the umpire refused to overrule the line judge and play simply continued. Serena was annoyed, but given she was dominating the match, turned the other cheek and went on to take the first set 6–2.

The second set went the other way, Capriati winning it 6–4 to set up the crucial decider.

In the very first game of that third set, Serena saved a break point on her serve before winning (so she thought) the next point with a beautiful passing shot. But as she got ready to serve for the game, she heard the umpire say: "Advantage Capriati."

Serena argued that it was her point, but the umpire was convinced, and the point was Capriati's giving her another break point. Serena saved it once again, but her mind was scrambled from her confrontation with the umpire and she went on to lose that first game.

It was in the final game of the match, with Capriati serving at 5–4 up that another three bad calls were made – all of them going in Capriati's favour. Everyone watching at home knew when a bad call was made as the television companies were using Hawk-eye for their replays, but that was of no use to the umpire or indeed Serena.

When Capriati served a double fault that went uncalled, even those within the stadium could see the umpire had got another one wrong. It was completely baffling.

In her post-match press conference Serena kept her cool and refused to blame inaccurate calls for her defeat, saying that she simply played badly. She received an apology from officials at the US Tennis Association though, who told her how much she meant to the tournament and to tennis. And the tournament director Jim Curley admitted that a video replay system for officials was likely to come into tennis at some point in the future.

It took a couple of years for the technology to make its Grand Slam debut, first appearing at the US Open in 2006, but now all the slams (barring the French Open) use it, as well as many other high-level tournaments.

It was a frustrating end to Serena's US Open and over time she came to realize that she could have handled the situation better. During the match she had allowed herself to get caught up in the feeling that she had been wronged, but when she reflected on it years later, she understood that the best way to deal with adversity is to rise above it. That by putting it to one side and moving on you give yourself the best chance of succeeding.

In the immediate aftermath she bounced back to win a tournament in China and made it to the finals of the WTA Tour Championships (a tournament held at the end of the season for the best eight players that year), where she suffered her second defeat to Maria Sharapova. A couple of months later the pair faced off again in the semi-finals of the 2005 Australian Open in a real thriller of a match that lasted two hours and thirty-nine minutes. Serena was three match points down in the third set, but gritted her teeth and battled back to win it 8–6 in an epic final set lasting sixty-six minutes.

In the final she faced world number one Lindsay Davenport. For both players it marked something of a comeback – Davenport hadn't been in a Grand Slam final since 2000, while Serena hadn't won a major singles title since Wimbledon in 2003. Neither was on top form in a final that swung first Davenport's way – with Serena leaving court at one point for treatment to a rib injury – and then Serena's. With the scores level at one set all Davenport appeared to run out of juice and Serena powered past her to take it 6–0.

Her seventh Grand Slam title took her back to number two in the world and Serena saw it as a good way to answer the rumours and suggestions that she and Venus had taken a step back from tennis. She insisted that there was nothing wrong and that the sisters were working really hard.

In reality there *was* something wrong. It just took Serena a while to realize it. She carried on playing that year, but the more she played, the more she resented playing. She withdrew from an indoor tournament in France with illness then retired from matches in Dubai and Amelia Island with injuries (one to her shoulder and one to her ankle). When she later pulled out of the French Open saying she had not yet recovered from her ankle problem it meant she had pulled out of more tournaments than she had won in 2005.

In the final five events she played that year Serena failed to even reach the quarter-finals.

# SERENA'S LAST FIVE EVENTS OF 2005:

**ITALIAN OPEN:** 2nd round defeat to Francesca Schiavone (world number 26)

**WIMBLEDON:** 3rd round defeat to Jill Craybas (world number 85)

**TORONTO:** 3rd round – withdrew with knee pain

**US OPEN:** 4th round defeat to Venus (world number 10)

**CHINA OPEN:** 2nd round defeat to Sun Tiantian (world number 127)

At the time, nobody knew what was wrong with the former world number one. It was strange to see her looking so fragile yet, when anyone asked her what was wrong, Serena would brush them off and insist everything was fine. She didn't allow herself to talk to anyone about how she was feeling – not her sisters or even her mum and dad.

Everything came to a head at the Australian Open in 2006. She was in the middle of a third-round match against the tall Slovakian Daniela Hantuchova when she suddenly became overwhelmed by a feeling she'd never really had on the court before: she didn't want to be there.

Eventually, during one of the changeovers it all came out. Serena started crying. Right there, in front of all the photographers and television cameras she could not stop the tears from rolling down her face.

Somehow, it escaped the eyes of the world watching, who put Serena's damp cheeks down to nothing other than the sweat of hard work.

She managed to keep on playing, but lost in straight sets. When she sat in front of the media after the match she told them she simply didn't play her best tennis that day: "I was hitting balls every which direction. I didn't feel any of them."

Serena headed straight back to Los Angeles, put her racquets away and didn't pick them up again for months. The official word put out was that she was suffering from a recurring knee problem, but in reality she was physically fine. Mentally and emotionally she needed some help.

She started having weekly sessions with a therapist. Talking to someone who had no links to her family or to tennis really helped her to understand why she was feeling so down and why, for the first time ever, tennis had become more of a problem than a solution.

Over the years, she and Venus had seen other girls burn out from tennis and always thought it would never happen to them. But since Tunde's death that had changed. Serena felt pressure to get back to playing tennis. She had signed a big contract with Nike while recovering after her knee surgery and felt a responsibility to them to get back on court too.

Instead of a joy, tennis had become a job. A way to keep other people around her happy.

It took time, but over the course of a few months something shifted in Serena's mind.

The way she later described it was that tennis had always been something that had chosen her, rather than the other way around. Yes, she had grown to love the game, but it had never been something she had made an active decision to spend her life doing.

Now, she had the opportunity to make that choice. She could choose tennis, if she wanted to. That ability to choose the sport on her own terms changed everything for Serena. She started to see it as a way to find herself again.

She made her return in late July, some six months after walking off court with tears in her eyes in Melbourne. Serena arrived for the tournament in Cincinnati not really knowing what to expect. She knew her fitness wasn't quite where it needed to be, but thought if she could play herself into shape it would be better than taking too much more time away from the tour. It might also stop her from sinking any lower in the rankings – she had already dropped to number 139, the lowest she'd been since she was starting out in 1997.

In her first-round match she played aggressive

tennis, aiming to keep the points as short as possible to avoid getting too out of breath in long rallies. And it worked! She beat the number two seed Anastasia Myskina in straight sets and went on to do the same in her next two matches. Her run came to an end in the semi-finals against Russian Vera Zvonareva, but she left Cincinnati with a good feeling. She was back playing again, and it felt right.

# GREAT EXPECTATIONS

From her low point of 139 in the rankings, Serena had climbed back up to number ninety-five by the end of 2006.

Runs to the semi-finals of a tournament in Los Angeles and the fourth round of the US Open suggested she was on the right path, but when the Australian Open rolled around at the beginning of 2007 she was not exactly back to her best.

She'd spent the end of 2006 visiting Africa with her mum and sisters Isha and Lyndrea. It was a trip she had wanted to do for a long time. She had always felt something drawing her towards the continent – like she was missing something by never having been there.

It turned out to be a trip she would never forget and one that truly helped to lift her out of the gloom that had consumed her since Tunde's death. The Williams women visited Ghana and

Senegal, putting on tennis clinics for kids in small towns and villages and giving out much-needed medical supplies like polio vaccines and malaria pills at local hospitals.

They also visited the notorious "slave castles" on the coast of Ghana. During the height of the transatlantic slave trade, enslaved African people were held there in dark, dismal dungeons before being loaded on to ships and sold in the Americas. It was an experience that left an indelible mark on Serena. She couldn't help but think about what her ancestors must have been through to survive such conditions; the journey to America and then whatever fate awaited them there.

It made her incredibly sad, but it also gave her a feeling of real hope and courage to know that she came from such strength. She was only here because her ancestors had survived so much and that gave her the feeling she could endure anything she came up against.

# TRANSATLANTIC SLAVE TRADE

- Beginning during the fifteenth century the Atlantic slave trade involved the transportation by slave traders of enslaved African people mainly to north and south America.
- Near the beginning of the nineteenth century, various governments acted to ban the trade, although illegal smuggling still occurred.
- The last recorded slave ship to land on American soil was the *Clotilde*, which in 1859 illegally smuggled a number of Africans into Alabama.

Serena returned to the WTA Tour with a renewed sense of purpose. Physically she was not as fit as she would normally like to be for the start of a season – it's not so easy to train every day when you're traveling around Africa.

So she arrived in Melbourne unseeded and, in the eyes of the media in particular, in no shape at all to be considered a contender for the title.

Serena did her best to block out the negativity. As an adult she had always been comfortable with how she looked. She knew she would never be one of the super-slim players on the tour because that just wasn't the way she was built. She had an athletic physique with strong arms and legs that had helped her to win seven Grand Slam titles, and she was proud of it.

If the press weren't expecting her to win then that was fine. She wasn't expecting to. Sure, she wanted to win, but she realized she was starting from a long way back compared to the other players. She saw the tournament as a way to close that gap before the next one came around.

There were other people who did place expectations on her though. Ahead of Serena's first match at the tournament she was visited by a representative from Nike – the company who sponsored her. His blunt message was that she needed to perform well in Melbourne, leaving her with the distinct impression that if she didn't, Nike might not be her sponsor for much longer.

Sometimes sportspeople are under more pressure than those of us on the outside ever really know about.

As an unseeded player Serena would have to beat six seeded players if she was to lift the trophy – a gauntlet that most thought would prove too much for her.

Her first "real" test was predicted to come in the third round against fifth seed and former world number three, Nadia Petrova. And for a time it looked as though Serena would fail. She lost the first set 6–1 and was 5–3 down in the second, just two points away from losing the match when she reminded herself of the words that her sister Venus had said to her ahead of the match: "Just look at the ball, and it'll come."

At that moment, it did. Serena's level went up a notch and she won the next four games in a row to take the second set 7–5. And any doubts over her fitness were scotched after she also won the third 6–3.

She battled through an even tougher quarter-final against Israeli Shahar Pe'er, winning it 8–6 in the third after more than two-and-a-half hours. And after a much swifter victory over Nicole Vaidišovà from Czech Republic in the semi-finals she was into her first Grand Slam final in two years.

It pitted her against the number one seed Maria Sharapova who, at the age of nineteen, had already won Wimbledon and the US Open. The build-up was full of expectations of a great final between two fierce competitors, but many thought beating the Russian would be a step too far for Serena.

It took her just sixty-three minutes to prove them wrong. Serena blew Sharapova away with her power and consistency winning the match and her eighth Grand Slam title 6–1, 6–2. The veteran television commentator and analyst Bud Collins described Serena's performance as, "one of the most improbable things I've seen in tennis." She had shocked the world, answered all the critics who had suggested her era of dominance was over and proved to herself that she was back where she belonged.

Amid her joy in lifting the trophy Serena gave the world a brief glimpse into her world away from the court when she ended her winner's speech by speaking about her sister Tunde: "I would like to dedicate this victory to my sister who is not here," Williams told the crowd as tears fell from her eyes. "Her name is Yetunde, and I just love her so much."

Serena's win in Melbourne rocketed her up the rankings to number fourteen. Although she didn't add any more slams to her record that year (Justine Henin knocked her out of the quarter-finals of all three!) she ended 2007 back within the top ten at number seven.

It wasn't until the following summer that she found herself back in contention for a Grand Slam title. She won tour titles in India, Miami and Charleston in the early part of the 2008 season, but lost in the quarter-finals of the Australian Open and suffered a surprise defeat to world number twenty-four Katarina Srebotnik in the third round of the French (by which time Serena was up to number five).

But then came Wimbledon and the US Open – two tournaments that elevated Serena back to the very top level.

She arrived in London as the sixth seed with Venus just behind her in seventh (Venus was the defending champion, having won her fourth Wimbledon title the previous summer). Ahead of them were four players who were all in contention for the world number one ranking: Ana Ivanovic, Jelena Jankovic, Maria Sharapova and Svetlana Kuznetsova. But one by one, they all fell away. By the time the quarter-finals came around not one of the four was left.

Venus and Serena were through. By the time the final came around it was once again Venus versus Serena for the Wimbledon singles title. The first Grand Slam final between them in five years marked something of a Williams renaissance, especially given the fact that a few hours after the final they would be back on court for the final of the women's doubles.

Before that though, Venus and Serena once again put sisterly thoughts to one side for a few hours as they exchanged powerful blows from either side of the net. Serena got off to a strong start, taking a 4–2 lead in the first set before Venus found enough momentum to get back on level terms at 4–4. With both sisters making very few errors, despite it being a gusty day on centre court, it looked as though the set was heading for a tiebreak. But serving at 5–6 down Serena faltered and that was all it took for Venus to take the first set after fifty-three minutes.

The battle was just as tense in the second set with a marathon third game lasting some fourteen minutes. Once again it was Serena who got the first break of serve, but, as in the first set, she was unable to hold on to the advantage. As the set went on it was Venus who seemed to get stronger. At 5–4 up she was able to get a timely break of serve to seal the match and win her fifth Wimbledon singles title.

Venus couldn't keep the smile from her face, but there was none of the joyous leaping around the court she would have allowed herself against any other opponent. Serena was clearly downcast and later admitted she was not satisfied with the way she played. But the match had been of such high quality (there were just thirteen unforced errors during the first set) that she couldn't help but draw some strength from it.

A few hours later, she and Venus went on to win the doubles final. It was their third doubles title together at Wimbledon and one that put them in the driving seat when it came to representing the USA at that summer's Olympic Games in Beijing.

## OLYMPIC GAMES

- The Olympic Games are a global multi-sport event held every four years.
- The first Olympic Games in ancient Greece is thought to have taken place in the eight century.
- Over 200 countries now participate in the Olympic Games including Greece, Australia, France, Great Britain and Switzerland.
- The famous rings on the Olympic flag

represent the solidarity between what used to be considered the five inhabited continents (counting the Americas as one continent) of the world. We now consider there to be seven continents: Asia, Africa, North and South America, Antarctica, Europe and Australia.

Olympic flag

Their second Olympic gold (after winning together at the 2000 Olympics in Sydney) was a proud moment for the Williams sisters. Both were left disappointed in the singles event this time though, Serena losing to Elena Dementieva in the quarter-finals and Venus to Li Na at the same stage.

Venus's Wimbledon victory had evened up the scores between the sisters at eight Grand Slam singles titles each, but there was still time for one of them to forge ahead before the year was over. It came at the 2008 US Open where Serena and Venus were listed as the fourth and seventh seeds respectively.

On Friday 22 August, Serena opened up her diary and wrote down exactly what was going through her head:

"I HAVE TO PLAY VENUS IN THE QUARTERS!!! ... I'M SO BUMMED ... WHY CAN'T I PLAY SOMEONE ELSE?"

When the number one seed Ana Ivanovic was knocked out in just the second round it meant that her spot at the top of the world rankings was potentially up for grabs. If Serena could make it past Venus and win the tournament, she would be back at number one – something that seemed almost impossible just two years earlier when she had dropped all the way down to 139.

Serena and Venus cruised through their early rounds making the first week of the tournament seem like one long warm up for another all-Williams match-up. When the day did finally arrive, an expectant crowd and television audience was made to wait even longer as rain delayed the start of the Williams sisters' clash from its scheduled 7 p.m. start to almost 9 p.m.

It proved to be well worth the wait. Over the course of nearly two-and-a-half hours Serena and Venus played out one of their most competitive matches yet; one that was packed with breathtaking tennis and dramatic twists.

It was Venus who seemed to be in control for much of the match, but when crunch time came it was she who faltered. Despite having two set points in the first set and eight in the second it was Serena who won the points when it mattered most and came out on top of two tiebreaks to win the match 7–6, 7–6.

"It felt like I was watching a really good movie – with me in it!" wrote Serena in her next diary entry. It was certainly a match to remember, but she still had two more to win if she was going to lift the trophy. Any time she knocked Venus out of a tournament before the final she felt it was her responsibility to go on and win it for both of them, because that's exactly what Venus would do.

With more rain falling in New York it took Serena a day longer than expected, but by late Sunday night she had her hands on a ninth Grand Slam trophy. Straightforward wins over Dinara Safina in the semis and Jelena Jankovi in the final had not only given her a third US Open title, but also elevated her back to the number one spot for the first time since 2003.

While everyone was congratulating her on the success, Serena was already talking about taking her slam count into double figures.

"...I FEEL LIKE THERE'S JUST

# SO MUCH THAT I CAN DO IN MY CAREER YET."

If anyone doubted her they didn't have long to wait before Serena backed up her words with some impressive actions. Over the next two years she added four more Grand Slams to her collection: two Australian Open titles and two Wimbledon crowns.

The French Open continued to elude her (she was knocked out in the quarter-finals in both 2009 and 2010). As did the US Open, which was perhaps more of a surprise given she had won it three times already. When she returned there in 2009, a year after that memorable quarter-final match against Venus, Serena was the favourite to win a second title in a row, but her campaign came to an abrupt and somewhat dramatic halt in the semi-finals.

Serena was up against Kim Clijsters, a former world number one who had just returned to the WTA Tour after a two-year break to give birth to her daughter Jada. Clijsters was unseeded and unranked going into the tournament, but by the time she and Serena met she had already got the better of one Williams sister, knocking Venus out in the fourth round.

The match was a close one and a real battle between two great competitors. Clijsters was edging it though, winning the first set 6–4 and leading 6–5 in the second when the match was overtaken by controversy. Serena was serving to try and take the second set into a tiebreak when at 15–30 down a lineswoman called "foot fault" on her second serve. Serena was not convinced she had faulted, but the umpire stuck with the call. That made the score 15–40, meaning Clijsters had two match points.

Serena was furious and said as much to the line judge who had called the foot fault. At that point the umpire called the line judge over and asked her what had been said, with Serena soon joining in the discussion. Moments later, to a background chorus of boos and whistles Serena threw her racquet into her bag and walked over to Clijsters to shake her hand.

The umpire had given Serena a code violation

for "unsportsmanlike conduct". Unfortunately for Serena it was her second of the match after she had received one for smashing her racquet after losing the first set. It resulted in a "point penalty" for Serena meaning that a point was awarded to her opponent. It just so happened that in this case that was a match point.

Two days later Serena released a statement apologizing for her behaviour. She apologized not only to her fans, but to the lineswoman, and to Kim Clijsters, for her outburst.

She was fined $10,000 by US Open officials in the immediate aftermath and later received a further fine of $175,000 from the Grand Slam Committee (though this could be reduced to $82,500 if no further offence was committed up to 2011).

## FOOT FAULT

The server must stand behind the baseline, between the centre mark and the sideline.
If any of the following happen before the ball is

hit then a "foot fault" is called:
- Feet touch the ground inside the baseline
- Feet touch the wrong side of the centre mark
- Feet touch the wrong side of an imaginary extension of the sideline

Just as with an ordinary fault on a serve, a player is given the chance of a second serve if a foot fault is called on their first serve.

# CODE VIOLATIONS

Players can receive these for a wide variety of misdemeanours including:
- Racquet abuse
- Audible obscenity
- Unsportsmanlike conduct
- Ball abuse
- On-court coaching
- Verbal abuse
- Time violations

It was a low point for Serena, but she was still able to finish the year on a high, winning the WTA Tour championships (a tournament where only the top eight players in the world compete for the title) and ending 2009 as the world number one. It had been her busiest season yet, playing in a total of sixteen tournaments.

# BACK TO BASELINE

Serena was flying high in the summer of 2010. She had won her twelfth and thirteenth Grand Slams in Australia and Wimbledon, and was looking ahead to a US Open where she was desperate to erase the bad memories of the previous year.

But then came a night she won't ever forget. It came a matter of days after her triumph at Wimbledon in July when she was in Munich with some friends. They had all been out for dinner and as they left the restaurant Serena felt a sharp pain in her foot. Looking down, she saw a pool of blood surrounding her feet.

Serena had stepped on some broken glass and suffered bad cuts to both her feet. At a Munich hospital she received eighteen stitches: six inside the cut on her right foot, six on top of that foot and six on the bottom of her left foot.

When she got back to the US she realized that something wasn't quite right: her big toe was drooping. A specialist quickly diagnosed that Serena had torn a tendon in her foot and needed surgery to fix it. Serena spent six weeks or so after the surgery wearing a protective boot before gradually getting back on the tennis court.

Her hope was that she would be fit enough to compete in the 2011 Australian Open. But her determination to get back into training as soon as possible ended up delaying her return even further. By October she was back in hospital for a second operation after putting too much pressure on the tendon and tearing it for a second time.

Announcing her withdrawal from the Australian Open in November Serena admitted that pushing herself back into intense training too early had only caused her further damage. But she made a promise to her fans that she would be back, "better than ever", as soon as she could be.

This time Serena spent ten weeks in a cast and a further ten weeks in a protective boot. She still found ways to get on the tennis court though – at one stage using a wheelchair to manoeuvre herself around so that she could hit some balls.

When she wasn't doing that, Serena was often singing karaoke at home with Venus – one of her favourite ways to relax.

By mid-February, Serena's boot had finally been removed and the tennis world was speculating on when they might see her back on the WTA Tour again. But all that chatter quietened down when it emerged that she had suffered a serious setback – not to her foot, but to her health.

It started shortly after Serena returned to LA from a trip to see her foot specialist in New York when she developed a swelling in her leg and was having problems with her breathing.

The doctors couldn't find anything wrong with her leg, but ordered a scan of her lungs that showed she had a pulmonary embolism; a clot that blocks blood flow to the lungs. Serena had several clots in both of her lungs. She was immediately admitted into hospital for emergency treatment and spent a few days there before being allowed home.

For the next few weeks she had to inject herself twice a day with blood-thinning medication to help treat the clots. But by the end of February she was back in hospital, this time with a large haematoma (or lump) on her stomach – a localized pooling of blood that's a common complication of the treatment she'd had.

This time, she left hospital with a blood-drainage tube emerging from the area of her stomach where the lump had been with instructions to take blood-thinning medication for at least three months.

Serena focused on being well enough to get back on the court, setting a rough target of being on the WTA Tour by the summer. Tennis was built into her psyche. It was part of her rebuilding process; once she was hitting balls again, she knew she was on the mend.

One of her doctors tried to warn her against it, saying: "If I were you, I wouldn't play again." Serena looked him right in the eye and responded: "You're not me." Challenges had always motivated her, and this was simply her biggest challenge yet.

Serena returned to the practice court in April under medical supervision. Her sessions were short to begin with, as she tried to build her fitness back up from probably the lowest starting point it had ever been. But gradually she got stronger and by late May she was back training at what she called "full strength".

She had already started preparing herself mentally for returning to Grand-Slam action at Wimbledon, but before she could confirm her return to the rest of the tennis world she had to get full sign-off from her doctor.

When the scans of her lungs came back showing no more blood clots, Serena couldn't help but shed a joyful tear. She was cleared to travel to the UK, but on one very important condition: she had to inject herself with the blood-thinning medication before she boarded the plane.

As soon as she had the all-clear, Serena released a statement to confirm she would be competing at a Wimbledon warm-up event in Eastbourne:

"I HAVE SO MUCH TO BE GRATEFUL FOR. I'M THANKFUL TO MY

# FAMILY, FRIENDS AND FANS FOR ALL YOUR SUPPORT. SERENA'S BACK!"

After almost an entire year away, Serena's first tournament back took place in the sleepy seaside town of Eastbourne. It was quite the wake-up call for everyone – even Serena took a little while to get going. In her opening match against Bulgaria's Tsvetana Pironkova she won just a single game in the first set, losing it 6–1. But instead of berating herself for playing badly Serena turned it into a positive, telling herself that a short first set meant she still had enough energy to build some momentum if she could start making her shots.

She did just that, winning the second set 6–3 before wrapping up the victory 6–4 in the third. Physically, there were signs that she wasn't at her best; she was moving slowly between points, receiving a warning for time violation from the umpire late on in the match, and later admitted that the breaks between changeovers felt like they were "five seconds long". But mentally Serena was clearly as tough as ever – arguably even tougher considering what she had overcome simply to be competing.

Serena was knocked out in the next round by Vera Zvonereva – the same player she had beaten to win Wimbledon twelve months earlier. But she left Eastbourne having shown everyone that her comeback was well and truly under way.

The following week, she returned for her first round match at Wimbledon – on the same court where she had won her thirteenth Grand Slam singles title twelve months earlier. She was up against the unseeded Frenchwoman Aravane Rezaï – a player renowned for her hard hitting. It was a tough match, with Serena winning the first set 6–3 before losing the second by the same scoreline. But in the third set she was able to break Rezaï's serve in the fourth game to go 3–1 ahead and took command of the match from there, winning the set 6–1.

After serving her final ace on match point, Serena was overwhelmed by emotions. She had tears in her eyes as Rezaï shook her hand at the net.

Speaking to the crowd on the court after the match Serena tried to explain the reasons for those tears, saying how tough of a year it had been, but that support of her family and loved ones, as well as the fans, had helped her immensely.

# "...I'VE LEARNED THAT YOU CAN NEVER TAKE ANY MOMENT FOR GRANTED."

Serena needed another three sets to get past Simona Halep in her second-round match, but then eased past Maria Kirilenko 6–3, 6–2 to put her into the fourth round of the tournament. To reach the quarter-finals she would have to get past ninth seed Marion Bartoli, a former Wimbledon finalist who had just reached the semi-finals of the French Open and won the tournament in Eastbourne.

Serena put up a strong fight. Bartoli needed five set points to win the opening set and in the second she squandered three match points when serving at 6–5 ahead. The set eventually went to a tiebreak with Serena saving a fourth match point before a huge Bartoli serve eventually wrapped up the match.

It was Serena's earliest exit from Wimbledon in six years and sent her ranking tumbling to number 169, but she left confident that she was improving every day. "I just can't sit here and be disappointed," she said afterwards. "For the most part, I can just use this as momentum going forward. I can only get better and that can potentially be really scary, because I can only go up from here and I can just do so much more."

Perhaps Bartoli should have taken that as a personal warning because in her very next tournament Serena beat the Frenchwoman to win her first title in over a year at the Bank of the West Classic in California. "I hated the triple digits," she later joked of her ranking, which rocketed up to number seventy-nine after her win over Bartoli.

And two weeks later Serena added another title, this one coming in Toronto where she beat the tenth seed Sam Stosur in seventy-seven minutes. It gave her another boost up the rankings to number thirty-one, just in time for the US Open where her form and history made her the most talked-about player in New York.

Even so, she was only given the number twenty-eight seed by the US Open organizers who stuck with their policy of following the rankings for their seedings (some tournaments are more flexible and take into account players' past performances). Serena's seeding meant she faced the possibility of playing one of the top eight seeds as early as the third round, and that's exactly what happened.

Serena was up against fourth seed Victoria Azarenka in the third round – a match that would not have seemed out of place as a semi-final or even final. Even so, Serena swept Azarenka aside in the first set, winning it 6–1 in just twenty-eight minutes. And when Serena held three match points at 5–3 up in the second it seemed as though she was on the verge of an impressively straightforward victory.

But Azarenka refused to yield. She saved all three match points to win the game and went on to break Serena's serve, ultimately sending the second set to a tiebreak. With Azarenka playing more aggressive tennis, Serena was pushed hard as she tried to wrap up the match, but on her fifth match point she hit a stinging return of an Azarenka serve that proved too much for the Belarusian, earning Serena a hard-fought victory.

Serena didn't need any more tiebreaks to reach the final, as she recorded a series of straightforward wins over Ana Ivanovic, Anastasia Pavlyuchenkova and Caroline Wozniacki. Up against the number nine seed Sam Stosur in the final, a player she had lost to just twice in six meetings, it seemed as though she was on course for a fourteenth Grand Slam title.

Stosur had reached the French Open final a year earlier, but she had never been beyond the third round at the US Open before or won a Grand Slam singles title. She was renowned for being physically very strong, but mentally fragile, perhaps lacking the self-belief needed to win a major title.

Rain delays earlier in the tournament meant that Serena's semi-final didn't take place until Saturday night. It was almost 11.30 p.m. by the time she secured her victory against Wozniacki and gone 4 a.m. by the time she fell asleep – not the ideal preparation for the Sunday afternoon final.

Serena certainly struggled in the first set. Her serve, which was usually one of her biggest weapons, was slower and far more wayward than usual; she only made thirty-five per cent of her first serves during the opening set. Stosur, meanwhile, was playing superb tennis, attacking Serena's flailing serves and making the most of her powerful forehand to great effect. The Australian wrapped up the first set in thirty-one minutes, becoming the first player to win a set against Serena in the tournament.

Stosur's dominance looked set to continue in the second set as she earned two break points on Serena's serve in the opening game. Serena saved the first one with an ace.

On the second, she unloaded a big forehand. Just as Stosur stretched to get her racquet to it, Serena let out a huge cry of "Come on!" thinking that she had just hit a winner.

Moments later the chair umpire announced that the point had in fact been awarded to Stosur, ruling that Serena's cry had hindered Stosur's ability to complete the point.

Despite Serena's protests and amid quite a bit of booing from the crowd, the break of serve was Stosur's.

Serena's frustration seemed to invigorate her for a time as she broke back immediately, but a few games later she was broken again and this time Stosur held on to her advantage.

## WHAT'S THE RULE?

International Tennis Federation rules say: "If a player is hindered in playing the point by a deliberate act of the opponent(s), the player shall win the point. However, the point shall be replayed if a player is hindered in playing the point by either an unintentional act of the opponent(s), or something outside the player's own control (not including a permanent fixture)."

With Serena serving at 3–5 down Stosur took a 40–15 lead, earning herself two championship points. Both were saved. But a big attack on Serena's serve gave her a third and this time she grabbed it, securing a huge upset to become the first Australian woman to win a major championship since Evonne Goolagong Cawley at Wimbledon in 1980.

It was a tough defeat for Serena to take. But she reminded herself that just six months earlier she had been in hospital wondering if she would ever be healthy again, let alone back in the final of a Grand Slam. It had been a remarkable comeback, but Serena wasn't calling it a complete one just yet.

Evonne Goolagong Cawley

## EVONNE GOOLAGONG CAWLEY

• The former world number one won her first Grand Slam title at the 1971 French Open when she was just nineteen.

• Born into an Australian aborigine family she grew up in a small farming village of around 900 people called Barellan, 360 miles west of Sydney.

- She was discovered playing tennis on the local dirt (clay) courts by an Australian tennis coach called Vic Edwards who invited her to live at his tennis school in Sydney where she stayed until turning professional.

- During the 1976 US Open (where she reached the final) she discovered she was pregnant with her first child and stepped away from the tour until the late summer of 1977.

- She came back to win ten tournaments including the Australian Open in a run of five consecutive tournament wins and reached the final in two others, including the season-ending WTA Championships.

- From being unranked at the beginning of her return, Goolagong's ranking rose to number three in the world.

- At time of writing she is the only mother to have won the Wimbledon title since Dorothea Lambert Chambers in 1914.
- It wasn't until Kim Clijsters won the US Open in 2009 that another female player returned to win a Grand Slam title after having a baby.

# NEW BEGINNINGS

**M**idway through her seventeenth season as a professional tennis player, Serena experienced something on a tennis court that she never had before: a first-round defeat in a Grand Slam tournament.

It came at the French Open in May 2012, some eight months after her run to the US Open final that had promised so much. The year hadn't started too well with Serena suffering an ankle injury in a tournament in Brisbane. Although she recovered enough to play in the Australian Open, she only made it as far as the fourth round before losing to Ekaterina Makarova, the lowest-ranked player left in the tournament.

After the match, former world number one Chris Evert, who now works as a commentator, said she had never seen Serena play so poorly in a Grand Slam match and questioned whether now she had hit the age of thirty, Serena was simply having, "more bad days, more flat days."

But when the clay-court season arrived in April, things started to click. Serena won tournaments in Charleston and Madrid and entered the French Open as one of the favourites for the title – even if she hadn't made it past the quarter-finals in Paris since 2003.

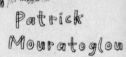

Patrick
Mouratoglou

Her first-round opponent was Virginie Razzano, a Frenchwoman ranked 111th in the world who had never made it beyond the fourth round of a Grand Slam before. Many expected a routine victory for Serena. Instead, the match turned into a three-hour drama with a twist that nobody saw coming.

Serena won the opening set 6–4 and when the second went to a tiebreak she raced to a 5–1 lead. She was two points from victory while Razzano was struggling with cramp in her thigh. The match was over. Surely.

Except it wasn't. From 5–1 down Razzano won

six points in a row to win the tiebreak and take the match to a third set. If that was a surprise, then what happened next was a shock of seismic proportions.

Razzano took the first five games of the deciding set, putting her on the brink of the biggest win of her career. But physically she was struggling and allowed Serena to claw her way back to 5–3. Then came an epic twenty-three-minute final game filled with thirty points – more than some sets contain! It featured five break points for Serena and seven match points for Razzano until finally, three hours and three minutes after they started playing, Razzano secured the victory on her eighth match point.

It was the first time in forty-seven first-round Grand Slam matches that Serena walked off court as the loser.

In the days that followed, Serena retreated to the apartment she owned in Paris (a city she loves) and thought about her next move. It led her to pick up the phone to a French coach called Patrick Mouratoglou, who owned his own academy on the outskirts of Paris and had coached a host of top-thirty players, including Grigor Dimitrov, Jeremy Chardy, Anastasia Pavlyuchenkova and Aravane Rezai. When Serena told him she needed somewhere to practise, he was more than happy to oblige.

She started to train there every day and started to build a strong relationship with Mouratoglou. They talked a lot about tennis and Serena's recent troubles on the court, particularly her defeat to Razzano. Mouratoglou was honest. He told her that she had appeared emotionally uptight and often unbalanced in her movement.

They got on so well that Serena asked him to travel to Wimbledon as part of her team – she wasn't ready to call him her official coach just yet, but it was a good opportunity to see how it might work out if things went that way.

For him, it was an eye-opening experience to see the attitude of a player who already had thirteen Grand Slam titles to her name: "Despite everything she has achieved, she still wants to improve. That's the most impressive thing," he told the media during the 2012 Wimbledon tournament. "She's unbelievable because she wants to get better every day, to progress and be better. But I've been told that champions are not people like others."

It proved to be a successful two weeks for Serena. Despite some nervous moments, including a 9–7 third set in her third-round win over China's Zheng Jie, she reached her seventh Wimbledon final, putting her one match away from ending her run of two years without a Grand Slam title.

To do that she would have to beat the world number three Agnieszka Radwanska, the first player from Poland to reach a Grand Slam final since 1939. It certainly seemed as though it was Serena who settled into the match the quicker of the two as she swept up the first set 6–1. When she took a 4–2 lead in the second it seemed as though the match might be over before Radwanska had even had the chance to settle in.

But with the trophy within touching distance, Serena was suddenly the one who started to look nervous. Her movement, which had been so fluid for almost two sets, slowed and the errors crept into her game. All of which gave Radwanska the chance to get herself into the match. She gratefully took it, winning the second set 7–5.

The deciding set was a tight, tense affair to start with, but when Serena served four straight aces to take the score to 2–2 it seemed to flush out any nerves that were left in her system. In the very next game she broke Radwanska's serve and was soon serving for the match at 5–2.

The moment she hit a backhand winner at 40–15 to wrap up the title, Serena's emotions came flooding out. She fell to the ground and lay flat on her back, covering her face with her hands as she thought of everything she had been through since the last time she had won a trophy on that very court.

After jumping into the crowd to celebrate with her parents and sisters Venus and Isha, Serena stood on the court to receive her trophy and told the crowd what it meant to her to be winning Grand Slams again:

"I ALMOST DIDN'T MAKE IT A FEW YEARS AGO IN THE

# HOSPITAL. I NEVER DREAMED OF BEING HERE AGAIN. NEVER GIVE UP — YOU CAN ALWAYS CONTINUE."

By picking up her fifth Wimbledon singles trophy Serena had equalled Venus's haul at the tournament, something she made sure to mention before leaving the court:

# "I'VE ALWAYS WANTED EVERYTHING VENUS HAS, SO ... I HAD TO COPY YOU AGAIN, SORRY!"

## SERENA'S RECORD-BREAKING WIMBLEDON WIN

- By winning the 2012 tournament Serena became the first female player over the age of thirty to win the Wimbledon title since Martina Navratilova in 1990.
- She set a record for most aces served in a tournament, hitting 102 aces which was the most of men or women at the Championships that year.

But even with fourteen Grand Slam titles to her name she was still hungry for more and told the media that she was going to be playing for many, many more years.

"TENNIS IS WHAT I HAVE AND I KNOW I'M GOOD AT IT. IT'S ONE THING THAT

I CAN RELY ON, IT NEVER REALLY LETS ME DOWN AND I CAN DO SO MUCH WITH IT. I REALLY APPRECIATE EVERYTHING THAT I HAVE."

With the words of former world number one John McEnroe ringing in her ears: "I believe we're watching the greatest female player that's ever played this game", she took her Wimbledon success and simply carried on winning. Before the end of the year she played in five more tournaments and only failed to win one of them.

At the 2012 Olympics in London, the tennis event was held at a location Serena was pretty familiar with: Wimbledon. She showed just how comfortable she was there by steamrolling her way through the Olympic tournament, dropping just a handful of games in each match en route to the final against Sharapova. Even that match only lasted one hour and three minutes, with Serena brushing the Russian aside 6–0, 6–1.

Winning Olympic gold made Serena just the second woman (after Steffi Graf in 1988) to win a "Career Golden Slam", meaning she had won all four slams and an Olympic gold medal.

On top of this, Serena's fourth US Open title came shortly after the Olympics, along with a win at the season-ending WTA Championships. All this makes it obvious that at the age of thirty-one (as she was by the end of 2012), Serena was still dominating the women's game.

The US Open victory that took her to fifteen Grand Slam titles came on the very same court where she had won her first major title some thirteen years earlier. Back then, it was her dad Richard guiding her along the way. By the time she collected number fifteen he had become more of a background figure, with Mouratoglou now in position as her official coach.

The partnership was clearly working and although Serena will always refer to her dad as the most important person in her career, she also recognized that the time had come to make a change: "When you've been playing professional for fifteen years, you need a change sometimes. It's almost like I'm starting over. When you first come out on tour, you have so much excitement and you're so hungry because everything is kind of new. I feel like it's all coming back like that for me."

## GOLDEN GIRLS

• With Serena becoming Olympic champion at London 2012 and also winning gold in the doubles with Venus, the sisters had become the only players ever to have won four Olympic gold medals in tennis:

• Venus: singles gold in 2000

• Serena: singles gold in 2012

• Venus & Serena: doubles gold in 2000, 2008 and 2012

Despite Serena's success in 2012, she finished the year ranked number three in the world behind Azarenka at number one and Sharapova at number two. But the ranking wasn't something she was too focused on, preferring instead to think about winning titles and slams. Besides, she was confident that the number one spot would come again eventually.

Once again, she was right.

In fact, it only took until February 2013 for Serena to reclaim the top spot, which she had last held in October 2010. It came after her first three tournaments of the year, which included a win at the Brisbane International, a run to the quarter-finals of the Australian Open (where she was hampered by ankle and back problems) and a runner-up spot at the Qatar Ladies Open in Doha.

Serena's defeat in the Qatar Ladies Open came to Azarenka – the very same player she was about to replace as world number one and an opponent she had beaten the last nine times they'd played. She was disappointed to miss out on the title, but the number one spot made it slightly easier to swallow.

Of her disastrous year out with the foot

injury and then blood clots, she said:

# "THERE WERE OFTEN TIMES THAT I NEVER THOUGHT I WOULD PLAY AGAIN."

At the age of thirty-one, Serena had become the oldest woman to reach the WTA's top spot.

## OLDEST WTA WORLD NUMBER ONES

- **Serena Williams:** 31 years, 4 months, 24 days
- **Chris Evert:** 30 years, 11 months, 3 days (Nov 24, 1985)
- **Martina Navratilova:** 30 years, 9 months, 29 days (Aug 16, 1987)
- **Lindsay Davenport:** 29 years, 7 months, 8 days (Jan 29, 2006)
- **Serena Williams:** 29 years, 0 months, 14

days (Oct 10, 2010)
- **Steffi Graf:** 27 years, 9 months, 16 days (Mar 30, 1997)

From then on, Serena seemed to move into a different stratosphere, leaving the rest of the field trailing in her wake. In the lead-up to the French Open she played in four tournaments – Miami, Charleston, Madrid and Rome – and won them all.

It had been eleven years since she'd won her only French Open crown in 2002, with the common assumption being that clay was the surface on which Serena was most vulnerable. But in 2013, she entered the tournament as the top seed and was determined to erase the nightmare of her first-round exit a year earlier.

By the time she reached the quarter-finals, no one was talking about the drama of twelve months before. Serena had lost a grand total of ten games in her first four matches and was blasting away anyone who stepped into her path. Her first challenge came against 2009 French

Open champion Svetlana Kuznetsova in the quarter-finals.

Serena had been beaten the last four times she'd reached that stage of the tournament, but when she breezed through the first set 6–1 it didn't look like there was any danger of a repeat performance. But Kuznetsova dug in and won the second set 6–3. It was the first set Serena had lost in the tournament and she was clearly a little in shock as she allowed Kuznetsova to take a 2–0 lead in the third set.

"I thought, 'Can't go out like this again'," Serena said after the match of the pivotal third and fourth games in which she held off three break points on her own serve and then immediately broke Kuznetsova's to get herself back on even terms. From there Serena took the next three games and closed out the set with a forehand winner and a loud: "YES!"

Serena had made her share of unforced errors in that match, but in the next one she almost reached perfection, defeating Italian Sara Errani 6–0, 6–1 in just forty-six minutes. It was so impressive that legendary former player Chris

Evert described it as, "The best clay-court match I've ever seen from a woman. She was hitting winners from every angle of the court. Coming to the net. Drop-shotting. Volleying. She kept her concentration the whole game. I thought it was perfect and flawless."

The final pitted Serena against the number two seed and defending champion Maria Sharapova, a player she hadn't lost to since 2004. Given that record it turned out to be a more competitive match than some predicted, with Sharapova even breaking the formidable Serena serve in the first set. But Serena was playing on a level that no one could touch – even if she was clearly more tight and tense in the final than she had been throughout the rest of the tournament. After wrapping up the first set 6–4 Serena found herself serving for the championship at 5–4 ahead and on match point, smashed down her fifth ace in her last seven service points to finally win her second French Open title.

Throwing her arms high in the air, she did a little pirouette before falling to her knees and pumping her fists in delight. It was a title that she had wanted back for so long and one that tasted so much sweeter after the pain of her early exit the previous year.

Serena's win made her just the fourth woman in the Open Era to win each Grand Slam on at least two occasions, the other three being Martina Navratilova, Chris Evert and Steffi Graf. At the age of thirty-one she seemed to be at the top of her game, but when a reporter asked her in the post-match press conference whether she had thought about "retiring at the top" she gave an ominous response accompanied by a wide smile:

## "I WANT TO GO OUT AT MY PEAK, THAT'S MY GOAL. BUT HAVE I PEAKED YET?"

## GRAND SLAM RECORDS (AS OF JUNE 2013)

Serena's sixteenth Grand Slam title moved her to within two of the eighteen won by

Navratilova and Evert who were joint fifth on the list of women's Grand Slam singles winners. Serena has since gone on to win seven more Grand Slam singles titles, putting her second on this list with 23:

1. Margaret Court: 24 titles
2. Serena Williams: 23
3. Steffi Graf: 22
4. Helen Wills: 19
5. Martina Navratilova: 18
5. Chris Evert: 18

Before the year was up, Serena played her part in one of the biggest shocks of the Wimbledon fortnight, losing to Germany's Sabine Lisicki in the fourth round. Serena had gone into the tournament on a thirty-one-match winning streak and was not only the number one seed, but the defending champion. The expectation was that she would – at the very least – reach the final.

But the big-hitting German came through a match that Serena had numerous chances to win.

After losing the first set, Serena had come back to win the second 6–1 and then took a 3–0 lead in the decider, but she kept letting her advantage slip and Lisicki was ready and willing to keep on closing the gap.

After losing the final set 6–4, Serena admitted she "couldn't be more disappointed" and was heading back to the practice court to figure out how to win the match next time. Her coach Mouratoglou took a philosophical view of the defeat saying it was simply a reminder that, "Serena is human. You cannot expect for anybody, even if she is the greatest player of all time, to be perfect on all the matches all the year. She is not and she will never be. I think still that her low level is better than it was before. But she is a human. She is going to lose some matches and we have to be ready for that."

"Some", but not many. Not in 2013, anyway. In fact, Serena lost just one more match that year, losing the final of the Western & Southern Open in Cincinnati to Victoria Azarenka (although even that defeat was by a tiebreak in the third set; the narrowest of margins).

Outside of that loss Serena added five more titles to her record, including the US Open. She faced a real fight for her fifth title there though. The final saw her take on Azarenka once again and for the second time in a matter of weeks the pair became engaged in a battle that showcased the best of women's tennis.

After winning the opening set 7–5, Serena took a 4–1 lead in the second and twice served for the match. But Azarenka kept her cool and took advantage of Serena's growing frustration with the effects of the gusty wind swirling around Arthur Ashe Stadium, coming back to win the second set tiebreak.

The final set was something of an anti-climax after the first two with Azarenka fading while Serena only seemed to get stronger. And when she closed it out 6–1 to secure her seventeenth Grand Slam title, she leapt high in the air in delight, as if to show just how much more energy this near-thirty-two-year-old had left in the tank.

Despite the fact she already had eight titles to

her name in 2013, before the US Open – making it one of her most consistently successful seasons yet – Serena said after the final that she would not have been satisfied if she'd failed to add another slam to the list. "I felt almost disappointed with my year, to be honest," Serena said. "Yeah, I won the French Open, but I wasn't happy with my performances in the other two slams and not even making it to the quarter-finals of one. I definitely feel a lot better with at least a second Grand Slam under my belt this year."

Before she hung up her racquet for the year, Serena added another two titles to her 2013 record, winning the China Open and the season-ending WTA Championships. That took her total to an incredible eleven titles for the year – the most since Martina Hingis won twelve in 1997. Such success obviously comes with financial rewards too and by winning so many tournaments Serena had become the first woman ever to break the ten-million-dollar mark in prize money in a single year.

Her total of $12,385,572, eclipsed the previous single-season prize money record of $7.9 million set in 2012 by Victoria Azarenka. It was also just a whisker shy of the top earning men's player Novak Djokovic who earned $12.6 million that year.

The money wasn't a main motivator for Serena though. It was just something that came as a result of doing what she loved the most: winning.

"I think my dad got me into tennis because of the money," she said after her US Open win. "But me being naïve and silly, I never thought about it. I just thought, I want to win. I want to do what Venus does."

## 2013 IN NUMBERS

**13** finals reached

**11** titles won

**5** titles won on clay giving Serena a 28–0 record on the surface

**34** matches – the longest winning streak of her career (broken by her defeat at Wimbledon)

**95.1%** – the highest winning percentage of any woman since 1990

Serena finished the year as world number 1 for the third time in her career

# FORGIVENESS AND FIRSTS

What does the number eighteen mean to you?" the journalist asked Serena.

"It means legal to do some things," she replied, laughing. But seconds later her expression took on a more serious tone; one that showed it was a question to which she had given some thought.

"It also means legendary," she added.

Serena's eighteenth Grand Slam, equalling the haul of both Martina Navratilova and Chris Evert, had been on her mind ever since she'd won her seventeenth at the 2013 US Open. Maybe it had been on her mind too much because in the first three slams of 2014 Serena had failed to make it any further than the fourth round.

Sure, she'd won titles. She started the year by winning one in Brisbane. But then at the Australian Open she'd been knocked out in the fourth round by Ana Ivanovic – a former world number one, but also a player who had never beaten Serena and had only made it to one Grand Slam quarter-final since 2008.

After her defeat it emerged that Serena had been hampered by a back injury that was so bad she "almost didn't play". So perhaps it was nothing to get too concerned about, and besides, there were still three more slams to come.

By the time of the French Open, Serena had won two more titles, in Miami and Rome. But she had also been struggling with a thigh strain that forced her to pull out of the Madrid Open where she had reached the quarter-finals. In spite of her body seeming more fragile than it had in a while she was deemed as one of the favourites to win what would be her third title in Paris.

"I am going on adrenaline at the moment, so I'll take a couple of days off," she said, after lifting the trophy in Rome a week before the start of the French Open. "I hope to win one more Grand Slam before I retire, but I don't want to look too far ahead. There are hundreds of players who want to do the same."

It was perhaps an attempt to dampen the expectations around her, but it also offered a glimpse of the frustration she was feeling at a body that seemed determined to betray her dream of winning that magic eighteenth slam.

In the end it only needed to survive until the second round. That was when Serena came up against Garbiñe Muguruza – a twenty-year-old appearing in only her second French Open. With no victories against any player ranked within the top eight, Muguruza was a big underdog against the defending French Open champion. But she didn't play like it, taking just sixty-four minutes to beat Serena 6–2, 6–2.

It was the most lopsided defeat Serena had ever suffered at a Grand Slam. She offered her compliments to Muguruza afterwards, telling her that if she continued to play that well, she could win the whole thing. In front of the media Serena dismissed it as "one of those days", saying, "You can't be on every day, and gosh, I hate to be off during a Grand Slam."

A few weeks later Serena was trying to make sense of another early exit, this time from the third round of Wimbledon. Her defeat to twenty-fifth seed Alize Cornet came as yet another shock, particularly after Serena had cruised through her first two rounds, dropping just five games. She also won the first set against Cornet 6–1 before the match took a turn no one was expecting, not least the Frenchwoman sharing the court with Serena.

"I just cannot believe it," Cornet said in a television interview, as she came off the court after winning the last two sets 6–3, 6–4 to knock out the winner of five Wimbledon titles. "A few years ago, I couldn't even play on the grass, I was so bad. And now I beat Serena."

Tears of frustration dampened Serena's eyes during a final set in which her mental and physical powers seemed to disintegrate. It was tough to take, especially as she had worked so hard coming into the tournament. But she consoled herself with the thought that while her hard work might not have paid off at Wimbledon, that didn't mean it wouldn't have an impact further down the line.

Her early exit gave Serena the opportunity to take some time away from tennis. She needed to find a way to relax and not dwell on her disappointment, so she took a holiday, travelling with her hitting partner Sascha Bajin to his home country of Croatia.

On her return, she played the Bank of the West Classic in Stanford – a tournament she'd won the last two times she'd entered. While there were signs all week that her confidence was still fragile, she came through each of the tests she faced. Up against Angelique Kerber in the final she started slowly, going 5–1 behind in the first set before kicking into gear and winning six straight games to take the first set on a tiebreak. From there, Serena kept her focus and closed out the match with a 6–3 second set.

Getting back to winning ways was an important part of rebuilding herself mentally after the disappointment of Wimbledon. But she knew there was still plenty of room for improvement and used her next two tournaments in Montreal and Cincinnati to try and raise her level in time for the US Open.

In Montreal it was Venus who stopped her from reaching a second straight final, notching her first win over Serena for five years in the semi-finals.

But in Cincinnati no one could prevent Serena from lifting her fifth trophy of the season – not even an in-form Ana Ivanovic who Serena rolled over in straight sets in the final.

Among the most positive signs that her form was back was that she served twelve aces in that final. Her famously giant serve had been strangely absent at Wimbledon, but now it was back, just in time for the final slam of the year.

By the time she arrived in New York for the US Open, Serena was being talked about as one of the favourites for the title. But she didn't place any such expectations on herself. She had endured such a disappointing season, especially at the slams, that she felt the pressure on her was actually lifted. After failing to reach the quarter-finals in the last three slams, what more did she have to lose?

Right from her first-round match against fellow American Taylor Townsend it was obvious that Serena's decision to play without the weight of expectation that usually sat on her shoulders was the right one. Beating Townsend in fifty-five minutes Serena dropped just five points on her serve in the entire match.

The dominant, focused Serena was back, and she was making light work of every opponent she faced. After easing past Estonian Kaia Kanepi in the fourth round she allowed herself a moment of celebration in the on-court interview raising her arms in the air and exclaiming: "I finally made a quarter-final this year!"

She did more than that, reaching the final without dropping more than three games in a single set. The last obstacle standing between her and an eighteenth Grand Slam title was former world number one seed and one of her closest friends on the tour Caroline Wozniacki. On this occasion the Dane was no match for Serena who needed just an hour and a quarter to end her miserable year in the best possible way: with a sixth US Open title and the one that moved her level with Evert and Navratilova.

It was not until Wozniacki's final stroke went long that Serena finally allowed her true emotions to escape. Collapsing on to her back, she covered her face with her hands and started to cry. After so much disappointment and almost an entire year of answering questions about when and where number eighteen might come she had finally done it.

It took all of two hours and a bit after lifting the trophy for Serena to start talking about what was next. Number nineteen. It came at her very next slam – the 2015 Australian Open.

## WTA FINALS

- Serena ended the year by winning her third straight WTA Finals, becoming the first woman to do so since Monica Seles in 1992.
- The victory secured her a second consecutive (and fourth overall) year-end number one ranking.
- She'd held on to it for the entire calendar year; the first woman to do so since Steffi Graf in 1996.

Although 2015 would end up being a year of life-changing events for Serena, both on and off the court, it started in familiar fashion for a player who had already won five Grand Slam titles in Melbourne. Despite having to come from a set down to win both her third- and- fourth-round matches and dealing with a heavy cold for much of the tournament, Serena won her sixth Australian Open title by defeating Sharapova in the final.

Now the winner of nineteen slams Serena was level with Helen Wills Moody, with only two players ahead of her: Steffi Graf (twenty-two) and Margaret Court (twenty-four). It was an incredible feat and one that Serena allowed herself to reflect on in an emotional victory speech:

"GROWING UP I WASN'T THE RICHEST, BUT I HAD A RICH FAMILY IN SPIRIT AND SUPPORT AND STANDING HERE WITH NINETEEN

CHAMPIONSHIPS IS SOMETHING
I NEVER THOUGHT WOULD
HAPPEN ... SO ALL YOU GUYS
WHO WANT TO DO SOMETHING
OR BE SOMETHING, JUST
NEVER GIVE UP."

## HELEN WILLS MOODY

• An American tennis player who won
nineteen Grand Slam singles titles between
1923 and 1938 and held the
world number one position
from 1927 until 1933 and
then again in 1935 and 1938.

• She was the first
American female athlete

Helen
Wills
Moody

to become known globally, making friends with royalty and film stars.

- On the court she showed little emotion which led an American sportswriter to give her the nickname: "Little Miss Poker Face".

- In her autobiography she explained:

"I HAD ONE THOUGHT AND THAT WAS TO PUT THE BALL ACROSS THE NET..."

A few days after lifting the trophy in Melbourne, Serena made an announcement that resulted in sports headlines around the world: for the first time in fourteen years she was returning to Indian Wells. Serena had refused to play there ever since the 2001 tournament when an angry crowd booed and jeered her throughout her final against Kim Clijsters.

She had found it too difficult. Too difficult to forget the hours she spent crying in the locker room after the match and the feeling that she might have won the trophy, but she had lost the more important fight that day: the one for equality.

So, she had stayed away. Despite the annual questions and attempts by WTA officials to change her mind, she was adamant that the tournament had brought the Williams family too much pain for her to go back.

But in February 2015, she wrote a piece for Time magazine, explaining that she felt the time had come for her to return to Indian Wells. She also stressed the importance of forgiveness.

Serena had grown and learnt so much since her 2001 match at Indian Wells. She had come so far and had nothing to prove, She was ready to forgive, and hoped that the fans and institution had grown too.

Nelson
Mandela

## NELSON MANDELA

● It later emerged that Serena's decision
had partly been inspired by reading Nelson
Mandela's book. Before becoming President of
South Africa, Mandela had been imprisoned
for attempting to overthrow the country's
apartheid rule. He spent twenty-seven years

in jail before his release in 1990 when he emerged with one aim: to continue his fight against inequality and injustice and rescue a country that was on the brink of civil war.

- When that entailed working with the very same people who had kept him behind bars for so long, he did just that, refusing to allow any temptation for vengeance to stand in the way of what was most important to him. Mandela's capacity to forgive united South Africa and showed the world how powerful it can be.

While Serena was looking forward to laying the ghosts of the past to rest, there were also elements of doubt in her mind – what if she walked out on to court and the Indian Wells crowd booed her all over again?

As she emerged from the locker room for her opening match against Romania's Monica Niculescu, Serena nervously slipped off her headphones to hear the crowd. This time the noise they were making was a positive one. She breathed a sigh of relief and raised a hand in acknowledgement of the support.

By the time she reached her chair, Serena was in tears. After the match, she admitted that she hadn't really known if it was the right thing to do.

Serena made a nervous start to the match, losing the first two games to the world number sixty-eight, but an hour later she had won the first set to a chorus of cheers. When she closed out the match another hour later, she clenched her fist and waved to the crowd. Once again, she struggled to hold back the tears.

After the match, she said:

**"I FEEL LIKE I'VE ALREADY WON THIS TOURNAMENT," SHE SAID AFTER THE MATCH..."**

Nevertheless, as Serena made her way through the rounds it started to look as though the real trophy might be heading her way. But hours before she was due on court for her semi-final match against Simona Halep the news broke that Serena would not be playing. She had suffered a knee injury that made it painful for her simply to walk.

Serena had not made the decision lightly. She'd spent the previous two days trying to find a way to ease the pain enough so that she could play through it, but nothing was working. She even had an injection in her knee to try and take the swelling down, but that wasn't effective either. Eventually she had to admit defeat.

Withdrawing from the tournament was the last thing Serena wanted to do, given the drama that had followed Venus's withdrawal fourteen years earlier. But the pain was too bad and with the French Open on the horizon she couldn't risk making it any worse. She decided that the best way to do it was to explain to the crowd in person why she was pulling out.

Shortly after the conclusion of the first semi-final between Jelena Jankovic and Sabine Lisicki, Serena walked out on to court together with the stadium announcer. Many people in the crowd had already heard about her withdrawal via social media and as Serena was invited to speak, a few scattered boos could be heard in the distance.

"A couple of days ago," she started, "at my practice I injured my knee and I fought through it and I kept playing. And today, I was just struggling to even walk, and it was really sad because just four months ago I decided to start this journey to come back here at a place I've had so much success.

"It's been a wonderful journey, and I have to say that I'm so excited to have been able to come back here and start to build so many new memories, and I can only promise to come back next year and play right here on this court in front of you guys."

Her words were greeted mostly by cheers. There were still a few audible boos fighting to be heard, but for Serena it no longer mattered. Her return to the tournament had helped her to leave the bad memories behind and start filling the void with good ones. She had made her peace with Indian Wells.

The release seemed to have a positive impact on Serena. She went on to win the Miami Open and reached the semi-finals of the Madrid Open before suffering her first defeat of the year to Petra Kvitova. Her final stop before the French Open was in Rome where she was the two-time defending champion. But after easing through her first match Serena pulled out of the tournament with an elbow injury, conscious that continuing to play could affect her chances at Roland Garros.

## "...THIS ISN'T ABOUT QUITTING, IT'S ABOUT MAKING A BETTER DECISION."

But her time in Rome was not wasted. It would turn out to be one of the most important weeks of her life, for that was when she met Alexis Ohanian; the man who would later become her husband. The pair met in a hotel when Alexis sat at a table close to where Serena was having breakfast on the morning of her first match that week. He later admitted to never having watched a tennis match – on television or in real life: "I really had no respect for tennis."

Fortunately, that would soon change.

Their first date took place a few weeks later in Paris, before the French Open got under way. They spent six hours walking around the city Serena loved so much and getting to know each other. It was the beginning of a relationship that would alter the course of her life for ever. But not just yet...

Before then, Serena had a tournament to focus on and was heading into it without having won a warm-up tournament and with a multitude of injuries plaguing her year so far. On top of that, she came down with the flu after her third-round win over Victoria Azarenka.

Nevertheless she battled on and reached the final, having to come from a set down in four of her matches along the way – something she had never managed before at a Grand Slam. Instead of following her matches with an ice bath for recovery, she was sitting with her head over a steamy bowl of decongestant and drinking litres of orange juice in a bid to try and get over her illness.

And instead of spending the day before the final on the practice court, she spent it mostly in bed, wrestling with the thought of pulling out.

Fortunately, she did no such thing and managed to pull through her fifth three-set match of the tournament to win her twentieth Grand Slam title, beating first-time Grand Slam singles finalist Lucie Safarova 6–3, 6–7, 6–2. Still coughing and sniffing as she spoke to the media after her win, Serena explained how she was able to keep pulling herself back into matches despite her illness:

## "I REALLY WANTED IT. I WANTED IT SO BAD."

Winning the first two majors of the year started talk of whether Serena would be able to win a "calendar Grand Slam", meaning to win all four within the same calendar year. Her coach Patrick Mouratoglou admitted it was definitely one of the most difficult things to do in tennis

– but it wasn't impossible. And this was Serena after all.

## CALENDAR GRAND SLAM

It has been achieved six times in tennis history. On the women's side, Maureen Connolly (1953), Margaret Court (1970) and Steffi Graf (1988) have pulled the feat off. On the men's side Don Budge (1938) and Rod Laver (1962 and 1969) have done it.

# 'STILL I RISE'

On the first Friday of Wimbledon 2015, Serena found herself two points away from defeat. She was up against the home favourite, Heather Watson, who was playing the match of her life and had Serena firmly on the ropes in the third set of their third-round match.

"I honestly didn't think I was going to win," Serena said later. "I was thinking, what am I going to do tomorrow, find a dance class, hang around to watch Venus play?"

"How I pulled through, I really don't know. I just was like, 'Listen, if I'm going to go lose, I'm going to lose trying to do the right things.'"

So narrow are the margins between victory and defeat however that it took just ten minutes for the world number one to turn the tables completely, leaving fifty-ninth ranked Watson wondering how the match had slipped so swiftly from her grasp.

A week later, Serena was through to her eighth Wimbledon final, having defeated three former number one players along the way: Venus, Victoria Azarenka and Maria Sharapova. She was also within touching distance of completing her second career "Serena Slam", meaning she would hold all four Grand Slam titles at the same time.

Serena's opponent in the final was Garbine Muguruza – the Spanish player who had inflicted a heavy defeat on her in the second round of the French Open in 2014. This time the twenty-one-year-old was very much on Serena's turf; playing in her first slam final against a woman for whom reaching major finals had been an almost yearly occurrence for sixteen years.

Muguruza put up a good fight, but it was not enough to halt the steam train that was Serena at Wimbledon that season. Three years had passed since she had last lifted the winners' trophy on centre court and Serena later admitted that at the start of the year, "This was the one I really wanted to win."

At the age of thirty-three (soon to turn thirty-four) Serena's sixth title at the All England Club made her the oldest Wimbledon champion in the Open Era. But as far as the media were concerned, that was not the main headline to emerge from Serena's victory. Nor was it even the fact that her twenty-first Grand Slam put her just one behind Steffi Graf, whose twenty-two were the most won by a female player in the Open Era.

All they really wanted to talk to her about was the fact that she was now one slam win away from the ultimate tennis achievement: the calendar Grand Slam.

"You better ask all your questions about the Grand Slam, because it will be banned soon," Serena told a group of reporters shortly after her victory. She laughed, but it was a little insight into the pressure she was already feeling. For the first time since Steffi Graf in 1988, a player would be arriving at the US Open with three of the four slams under her belt.

Serena was on the brink of making history.

She arrived in New York fresh from another tournament win, this one in Cincinnati, where her fifth title of the year had come via a hard-fought win over Simona Halep. There had been a couple of worrying moments since her Wimbledon victory though, the first coming four days after the final, when she withdrew from the Swedish Open with an elbow injury – an injury that also stopped her from playing at the Bank of the West Classic where she would have been the defending champion. A few weeks later she suffered her second defeat of the year, losing in the semi-finals of the Canadian Open to eighteen-year-old Belinda Bencic.

But beating Halep in Cincinnati put her back on track and seemed the perfect way to lead into a US Open on which so much rested. "I'm ready to start it, get it over with and be done and go on to the next event," Serena said on the eve of the tournament, revealing how tired she had become of talking and thinking so much about the feat ahead of her.

Just as it had at Wimbledon, her first major test came on the Friday of the first week when she dropped the opening set of her match against the world number 101, Bethanie Mattek-Sands. It took until late in the second set for Serena to find the form that put her a level above her opponent, but from then on it was one-way traffic and Serena quickly wrapped up the third set 6–0 to put her through to the fourth round where she eased past fellow American Madison Keys.

The quarter-finals pitted Serena against the most familiar of opponents: Venus. It was the twenty-seventh meeting between the pair with Serena having won fifteen of them to her sister's eleven, including a straight-sets victory at Wimbledon a few months earlier. For the first half an hour or so it looked as though their US Open meeting was heading in the same direction, as Serena made just two errors in winning the first set 6–2.

It was something of a surprise when Serena double-faulted to hand Venus a 3–1 lead in the second set – and even more so when she did it again later on, gifting Venus another break and leaving her to serve for the second set at 5–1. For the second time in the tournament, Serena was forced into a third set.

She was the one to get the early break this time though, and with her own serve back on track after its brief departure in the second set there was only one likely outcome. Serena's twelfth ace of the match finished the slightly lopsided match: 6–2, 1–6, 6–3.

Her immediate reaction was to pump her fists, but within seconds her expression had changed to one of dismay. If she was through to the semi-finals then that meant Venus was out – a combination of outcomes she never found easy to deal with. But the look on Venus's face said that she felt the opposite way: her younger sister was on course to make history and she could not be more proud.

Standing in Serena's way of reaching the final was Roberta Vinci, a player she'd not lost to in four meetings. In fact, Vinci was yet to even win a set against Serena. The Italian had been having a difficult season up to that point, dropping from a career-high ranking of number eleven to number forty-three by the time she arrived in New York, where she surprised herself by reaching her first major singles semi-final.

The media called it a "mismatch", even predicting a "slaughter" would take place on the tennis court when Serena and Vinci went head-to-head.

As it happened, it was not Vinci who ended up dead and buried, but Serena's hopes of achieving the Grand Slam. In one of the biggest upsets in tennis history, the Italian inflicted possibly the most painful defeat of Serena's career, coming back from a set down to beat the world number one 2–6, 6–4, 6–4.

Serena had looked nervous from the beginning, but when she managed to win the first set it seemed her nerves had settled. In the second though, Vinci's clever mix of spin and length started to frustrate her and a wayward forehand in the fifth game handed Vinci a precious break. She went on to close out the second set, prompting Serena to smash her racquet in despair.

While Vinci was playing smart, steady tennis with the freedom of someone who had nothing to lose, Serena looked constantly on edge and unable to keep her cool when it really counted. Yet when the match entered a third set it was still Serena who was expected to emerge as the winner, after all she had won eighteen of her nineteen three-set matches in 2015 ahead of the tournament.

This time though it was not to be.

## WILLIAMS VERSUS VINCI

| | |
|---|---|
| ACES: | 16:1 |
| WINNERS | 50:19 |
| UNFORCED ERRORS: | 40:20 |
| TOTAL POINTS WON | 93:85 |

"I think she lost her way, mentally," said Serena's coach, Patrick Mouratoglou afterwards. Serena denied feeling any pressure in her post-match press conference, but it was patently obvious to everyone watching that although Vinci had played the match of her life that day, Serena's toughest battle had been the one inside her own head.

Nine months of chasing history had taken a huge toll on Serena, physically and mentally. A few weeks after suffering her crushing first defeat of the year in a major tournament she released a statement saying she would not be competing again in 2015.

"I'M A FIERCE COMPETITOR. AND I WANT TO COMPETE AS WELL AS I CAN, FOR AS LONG AS I CAN."

Instead of tennis Serena filled her time with promoting her fashion line at New York's Fashion Week, gave a speech to 1,200 students at the University of Pennsylvania in which she talked about the example set by Black activists of the 1960s, and wrote an essay for *Wired* magazine encouraging Silicon Valley (an area of San Francisco that's home to 2,000 tech companies) to hire more women and minorities. She wrote about the fact she had opened two schools in Kenya and enforced a rule that at least forty per cent of the students had to be girls (sometimes in Africa they only send the boys to school), because "equality is important".

"TO THOSE OF YOU INVOLVED IN EQUALITY MOVEMENTS LIKE BLACK LIVES MATTER, I SAY THIS: KEEP IT UP. [...] WE'VE BEEN THROUGH SO MUCH FOR SO MANY CENTURIES, AND WE SHALL OVERCOME THIS TOO. "

# BLACK LIVES MATTER

- This is an international movement that campaigns against violence and systemic racism towards Black people.
- The movement began in 2013 in response to the fatal shooting of African-American teenager, Trayvon Martin, in February 2012. When the man responsible was found not guilty (it was argued that he shot Trayvon Martin in an act of self-defence) there were protests across many states of America and the hashtag #BlackLivesMatter was born on social media.
- It gained further momentum in 2014 after unarmed eighteen-year-old Michael Brown was shot dead by a white police officer in Missouri sparking more protests.
- Under the banner of the #BlackLivesMatter campaign more than 500 people from eighteen cities across America signed up for a "freedom ride" to the town where the shooting took place.

- With Black Lives Matter chapters now set up across the US it has become the twenty-first century version of the Civil Rights movement.
- The Black Lives Matter movement gained further momentum in 2020 after the death of George Floyd – an African-American man killed during an arrest in Minneapolis, Minnesota.

Black Power!

Using her platform and ability to reach so many people to speak up for others was something Serena felt passionately about. And it was one of the things she was rewarded for when she was named Sportsperson of the Year by the iconic American magazine Sports Illustrated (SI) in December 2015.

For a few reasons, the award was a huge deal. Firstly, only two other women had been the sole recipient of it (not honoured as part of a team or alongside a male athlete) since SI first started running the award in 1954: fellow tennis player Chris Evert in 1976 and runner Mary Decker in 1983.

Secondly, Serena was the first sole African-American woman to win the honour.

On the night she was given the award she made a speech that earned worldwide plaudits. It was inspirational, honest and gave us an insight into the character of a woman who had endured and overcome so many obstacles to become one of the greatest sportspeople in the world:

# "...IT DOESN'T MATTER HOW OLD OR HOW YOUNG YOU ARE, YOU CAN ACHIEVE ANYTHING THAT YOU SET YOUR MIND TO. I ALWAYS SAY, IF I CAN DO IT, ANYONE CAN DO IT."

Serena closed her speech by reciting part of a poem by her favourite poet, Maya Angelou, called "Still I Rise".

## DR MAYA ANGELOU

- Maya Angelou was a prominent American writer, poet and civil rights activist.
- She was also known for her acting, screenwriting and even dancing.

- Maya Angelou was born on 4 April 1928 in Missouri, USA and died 28 May 2014 aged 86.
- One of her most widely known poems, "Still I Rise", is from her famous collection titled *And Still I Rise*.

Maya Angelou

# AGAINST ALL ODDS

In the end it took Serena an entire year; twelve whole months of fighting, sweating and stressing before she was able to win her twenty-second Grand Slam.

In that time people started to ask whether it would ever come at all. Maybe Serena was done. After all, she was thirty-four years old – an age when most players are thinking about retirement, not setting records.

But it wasn't like she was missing the target by much.

She returned from her four-month break ready to put her US Open heartache behind her in Australia and cruised through to the final without dropping a set. There she faced German player, Angelique Kerber.

Kerber was appearing in her first Grand Slam final at the thirty-third attempt, while Serena was featuring in her twenty-sixth.

But it was Serena who played like the nervous first-timer making forty-six unforced errors including serving six double faults (and a low-for-Serena seven aces). Kerber meanwhile played a near-perfect match making just thirteen unforced errors and mixing up her game with brave drop shots to keep Serena on her toes.

She chased down every ball throughout a first set in which Serena made twenty-three errors, winning it 6–4, but lost the second 3–6 after Serena cut her error count down to just five. The deciding set swung Kerber's way first when she broke Serena's serve in the sixth game, but the defending champion broke back. Kerber remained positive though and took on Serena's serve once again.

With one final break of serve, the match and the championship belonged to Kerber, 6–4, 3–6, 6–4. It was Serena's first defeat in the finals of the Australian Open, her first defeat in a three-set Grand Slam final and the first time she'd been beaten in a major final since the 2011 US Open.

"She's human," said Serena's coach, Patrick Mouratoglou afterwards. "When you are a big favourite in a Grand Slam final, you are a bit nervous. If you're not, you are not normal."

Being a runner-up wasn't something Serena had experienced too much in recent years, particularly at the slams where she had won twenty-one and lost just four of her finals before losing to Kerber. But over the next few months it became a recurring theme for Serena. Straight after the Australian Open she lost in the final of Indian Wells and although she went into the French Open on the back of winning her first title of 2016 at the Italian Open, she would fall at the final hurdle once again in Paris.

Garbine Muguruza was her opponent this time – the player who had beaten her in the second round of the French Open two years earlier, but who Serena had beaten in straight sets in the 2015 Wimbledon final.

It was the twenty-two-year-old's first-ever clay-court final, but she showed no fear in taking on Serena's power and countered it with plenty of her own. In the end though it was a clever floated lob that won the title for Muguruza and left Serena with no choice but to raise her left hand to her racquet strings and applaud the performance of her opponent.

Serena had been beaten 7–5, 6–4 by a player twelve years her junior and one of her biggest supporters Billie Jean King was calling it a "changing of the guard" moment. Losing back-to-back slam finals wasn't something Serena had ever done before and it led to questions: was the quest for number twenty-two beginning to wear Serena down?

On the eve of Wimbledon, Serena dismissed the idea, saying that she simply focused on winning each slam as it came around rather than obsessing over the number. She also reminded everyone that she was more than tough enough to handle the pressure.

She needed every bit of that mental toughness over the next fortnight as she endeavoured to win her first Grand Slam title in almost a year. As early as the second round she looked on the verge of a shock defeat to fellow American Christina McHale.

Some ten years Serena's junior and ranked sixty-four players beneath her, McHale took the first set after a tense tiebreak, leaving the defending champion smashing her racquet into the ground in frustration. Serena used that fire in the best possible way in the second set, winning five games in a row to level the match at one set each. But McHale went a break up in the final set, at one point leaving Serena 0–2 and 15–40 down.

It was then she buckled, serving two double faults to hand the initiative back to Serena who grabbed it with both hands.

There were times when she was evidently struggling, but she was a warrior and refused to back down.

She didn't drop another set for the rest of the tournament. The final was a rematch of the match that she had lost to Angelique Kerber at the Australian Open, but this time the German found Serena in excellent form.

Her serve, in particular, was a key weapon that day and did not allow Kerber to gain a real foothold in the match.

## SERENA'S SERVE

• Against Kerber in the 2016 Wimbledon final Serena recorded thirteen aces. She won thirty-eight of forty-three first-serve points. She faced just one break point – at three-all in the second set, representing Kerber's only real opening – and shut the door with aces at **117 mph** and **124 mph**.

When Serena hit the forehand volley that won her the championship, she dropped her racquet and fell to the ground as if she'd been knocked out by a heavyweight boxer. Finally, she had won her twenty-second Grand Slam title, equalling the Open Era record set by Steffi Graf. And finally, she admitted how difficult it had really been to try and put the record out of her mind for the last year.

Of course, the next question she faced was about the final record she was yet to match; the all-time haul of twenty-four Grand Slams achieved by Margaret Court. So, was she already thinking about that target?

With the glow of her latest victory still fresh. "One thing I learned about last year is to enjoy the moment. I'm definitely going to enjoy this."

The rest of the year was frustrating for Serena, with shoulder and knee injuries restricting her to playing in just two more tournaments; the 2016 Olympic Games in Rio and the US Open. She was unable to compete at her best in either of those, returning empty-handed from Rio and losing in the semi-finals of the US Open to Czech player Karolína Plíšková.

But the year was a positive one in so many other ways for Serena. In March she had yet again shown her willingness to use the power of her own voice for the good of others when she responded to comments made by the chief executive and tournament director of Indian Wells Raymond Moore. On the day of the final (in which Serena took on Victoria Azarenka), he'd told reporters that he thought female tennis players were "very lucky", and that if he was one he would, "go down every night on my knees and thank God that Roger Federer and Rafa Nadal were born because they have carried this sport."

Serena lost that final to Azarenka, but in her press conference after the match she put aside her feelings of disappointment to set the record straight. Calling Moore's remarks "mistaken and very inaccurate", she pointed out how many people tell her that they don't watch any tennis unless they are watching her or Venus play, and that the women's final at the US Open in 2015 sold out before the men's.

Moore later apologized for his remarks and stepped down from his roles at Indian Wells, a tournament that has supported the payment of equal prize money to male and female players since 2009.

In November, Serena and Venus teamed up to open a community centre in their hometown of Compton named after their oldest sister. They wanted the Yetunde Price Resource Centre to help support residents whose lives had been affected by gun violence, just as theirs had so devastatingly when they lost Yetunde in 2003.

Serena said on a visit to the centre,

"AND SO WHEN WE BUILT THIS CENTRE WE WANTED TO BUILD A PLACE THAT RESEMBLED HER... SHE WAS THE ROCK OF OUR SISTERHOOD."

The year ended with Serena being whisked away on a surprise trip to Rome by her boyfriend Alexis. The destination? The hotel where they had first met over breakfast. And the plan? A proposal.

Serena announced the news to the world

with a poem which she published on Reddit – the social media website co-founded by her now fiancé.

She returned to the tour in January 2017, with a new piece of jewellery on her ring finger, but the same mission: to win number twenty-three and surpass Steffi Graf's record.

It was a mission that would take on a whole new dimension about a week before the tournament started. Serena had been practising hard after losing in the second round of her Australian Open warm-up tournament in New Zealand and noticed that physically she felt a little different. It was nothing she could put her finger on, but after she threw up, her good friend Jessica suggested she could be pregnant.

Initially Serena laughed it off, but a few days later she decided to check, just in case.

Much to her surprise, Jessica was right. Serena was shocked and confused. Could she still play the Australian Open? And what about Wimbledon? She really wanted to win her seventh title there that year.

After speaking to Alexis, Venus and her long-time agent Jill Smoller, she went to see a doctor who estimated that she was around three or four weeks pregnant (though it later emerged that he was off by around five weeks), and said there was no risk at all to the baby from her playing. As long as she stayed hydrated and listened to her body she would be fine.

And so, Serena began her Australian Open campaign with nobody outside of the five pof them knowing (not even her coach) that she had a little helper growing inside her. As each match went by it became increasingly clear that Serena was in the kind of zone where nothing and no one was going to stop her.

Alexis later said that he believes she went into each match determined to win it as quickly as possible in order to protect the baby and she did a good job – getting through every round in straight sets and without the need for a tiebreak.

It turned into a special tournament for the Williams family as a whole as Venus was enjoying something of a resurgence after a difficult few years with illness. In reaching her first Grand Slam final in almost eight years Venus ensured that the world was going to get another all-sister

Grand Slam final – something they had not seen since Wimbledon in 2009.

Serena described it as "a dream come true" to be playing Venus for the Australian Open title:

"NOBODY HAS BEATEN ME AS MUCH AS VENUS. WHATEVER HAPPENS WE'VE WON..."

It was always a special moment when Venus and Serena were on the court together, but this time it was doubly so as the sisters were bound by a precious secret.

For what would be the final time in 2017, Serena put everything she had into a tennis match. She angrily broke her racquet in just the third game. And throughout the match she yelled at herself to "fight!" It was a reminder not to allow her competitive edge to be softened by either the presence of her sister on the other side of the net or the secret her body was hiding.

It worked. Serena came through a competitive match to win 6–4, 6–4 and surpass Steffi Graf as the all-time leader in Grand Slam titles in the Open Era. She'd made history – in more ways than one. Serena looked almost shocked at what she'd done. Venus meanwhile was bursting with pride and held her sister in a long, emotional embrace when they came together at the net.

There was only the smallest of hints in Serena's victory speech as to what had been going on behind the scenes when she thanked her god Jehovah for getting her through the tournament which she described as "a tough one". Given her smooth run to the final and the challenges with illness and injuries she'd overcome to win slams in the past, most people will have been scratching their heads at hearing her describe the past fortnight that way.

## AGE AIN'T NOTHING BUT A NUMBER

• In winning the Australian Open at the age of thirty-five Serena became the oldest woman to win a Grand Slam singles title in the Open

Era, breaking her own record set at Wimbledon in 2016.

- She also secured her tenth major trophy since turning thirty – an age by which most great women's tennis players of the past had already retired.

A few months after she lifted the Australian Open trophy, everything became clear. Serena posted a picture of herself on Snapchat standing side-on to the camera with the words "20 weeks" written at the bottom of the image. The picture spread like wildfire around the world, sparking speculative headlines: "Could Serena Williams really be pregnant?"

A few hours later, her publicist put out a statement confirming that Serena was indeed expecting a baby in the autumn, but that she would be returning to the tour in 2018 – a promise that Serena insisted was included in the press release. There was no way she wanted anyone thinking this was the end of her twenty-two-year tennis career.

Serena Williams

After all, she would not be the first player to return to the tour after having a baby. Kim Clijsters had already done so, even winning three Grand Slam titles after returning. Serena's good friend Victoria Azarenka also came back after having her son Leo in 2016.

Serena was so excited to be having a baby, but it was also a little scary. What if she didn't come back as strong as she was before? What if she couldn't be the best mother AND the best tennis player in the world?

Stepping away from tennis for so long while she was pregnant was also strange. It was the longest time she had been away from the game since her dad had first taken her on to the public courts in Compton, and she missed it. Missed the competition. Missed the crowd. Missed being out on court and hearing people shout her name.

She started dreaming of coming back in time for the 2018 Australian Open.

Her coach Patrick Mouratoglou even recalls getting a phone call from Serena during Wimbledon, while she was at home heavily pregnant. She asked him to arrange a hitting partner for her in September. "But you are giving birth in September," replied Patrick.

"Yes, when I deliver, I want to start my training."

Patrick warned her that the doctors might not be so happy with that idea, but Serena was adamant.

Before hanging up the phone she left Patrick

with a warning of her own:

# "DO NOT UNDERESTIMATE ME."

Alexis Olympia Ohanian Jr arrived safely into the world on 1 September 2017. But around twenty-four hours later her mum was back in the operating room, after doctors found another pulmonary embolism in her lung and a blood clot in her leg. It was a scary few days for the whole family as the hospital did everything they could to get Serena healthy again.

When she was eventually allowed home, Serena found herself bedbound. Any thoughts of getting back on the practice court were pushed to the back of her mind. All she wanted was to be well enough to get out of bed and help take care of her little girl.

It was a difficult start to motherhood, but with time, and the love and help of her family, Serena gradually recovered. It helped that she had another target in mind: her wedding day which was set for 16 November.

By that time, Serena was already back on the tennis court. She'd only had a handful of practice sessions and wasn't serving yet, but the process of her return had at least begun.

In interviews she talked about why she was so set on getting back on the tour, revealing that, while she loved her life at home with Olympia, she still felt like there was more for her to do on the tennis court. A little more to add to her story.

She also wanted to see how her new life impacted on her tennis. Serena told *Vogue* magazine that when she's too anxious she loses matches, but that since Olympia had been born, she hadn't felt that anxiety anymore.

"KNOWING I'VE GOT THIS BEAUTIFUL BABY TO GO HOME TO MAKES ME FEEL LIKE ...

# I DON'T NEED THE MONEY OR THE TITLES ... I WANT THEM, BUT I DON'T NEED THEM. THAT'S A DIFFERENT FEELING FOR ME."

Her first match back came at an exhibition event at the end of December in Abu Dhabi. It was something of a dress rehearsal to see how she felt on the court with two weeks to go before the Australian Open and pitted her against strong opposition: the 2017 French Open champion Jelena Ostapenko.

When Serena came off court after the three-set defeat she told reporters she was still undecided on whether she would play in Melbourne. She wanted to make sure that when she returned to the tour, she was truly ready to compete for the biggest titles.

Five days later she posted an update on her Snapchat saying that she was not yet ready for tournament tennis and that she felt she still had some work to do. She said: "After performing in my first match after giving birth I realized that, although I am super close, I'm not where I personally want to be. My coach and team always said, 'Only go to tournaments when you are prepared to go all the way'."

It was March when Serena made her return to the tour at Indian Wells, a place where she had so much history. By then her ranking had dropped from the number one position she held after winning the 2017 Australian Open to a lowly number 491 meaning she would not be seeded and so could face a top-ranked player in the first few rounds.

It seemed unfair – a bit like she had left her job to go on maternity leave and returned to find she would have to work her way up from the bottom all over again.

Serena's return to Grand Slam tennis came at the French Open. By then, she had lost in the third round of Indian Wells to Venus and then in the first round of the following tournament in Miami to Naomi Osaka – a player in fine form.

Every match gave her more insight into what she needed to work on. And each tournament her goal was to play better than she had in the last.

But when the French Open organizers released their seedings for the tournament and once again Serena's name was not among them, it sparked an important discussion. Questions were asked about whether the WTA should have a rule allowing players returning from maternity leave to have the same ranking they did before they stepped aside. Should the sport really be making it so difficult for players to return after having a baby? What if Roger Federer or Rafael Nadal were ruled out with an injury for eighteen months – would they be unseeded when they returned to playing Grand Slams?

Serena said on US television show *Good Morning America*,

# "IT SHOULD BE UNDER REVIEW TO CHANGE THESE

# RULES. MAYBE NOT IN TIME FOR ME, BUT FOR THE NEXT PERSON."

Over the next few months the debate continued until finally, in December 2018, the WTA announced they would be changing the rules; from the start of 2019, they would allow a player returning from long-term injury or pregnancy to have their ranking frozen. And when they returned, they could use this special ranking for seeding purposes.

It was a rule that undoubtedly would have helped Serena had it been in place when she returned, and she was happy to see it come in so that other players would not have to experience the same things she had.

## NEW RULES FOR RETURNING MOTHERS

• Serena's return put the WTA's treatment of new mothers firmly in the spotlight. The changes they made were important in helping female players feel they could take time away to have a baby and not have to sacrifice their tennis career because of it. Now the rules state: a player who is out of competition for fifty-two weeks or longer may use her special ranking in twelve tournaments. If a player's special ranking would qualify her for a seeded position in a tournament, then she will be an "additional seed" in the draw.

Despite being unseeded for her return to Roland Garros, Serena was very much the headline act. Everyone was excited to have her back on the big stage and to see whether she would be able to complete a fairy-tale return.

Before she had even hit a single ball, Serena was the talk of Paris thanks to her eye-catching outfit: a black catsuit that she dedicated to all the mothers of the world:

"FOR ALL THE MOMS OUT THERE ... HERE YOU GO. IF I CAN DO IT, SO CAN YOU."

After her first-round win over Kristyna Pliskova, Serena said:

"I FEEL LIKE A WARRIOR IN IT, LIKE A WARRIOR PRINCESS..."

It was practical too. The compression element helped Serena's circulation, which was important given her history of blood clots.

After coming through three rounds of the French Open, beating the numbers seventeen and eleven seeds along the way, Serena was due to face Sharapova in a much-anticipated fourth-round match. Serena was improving with every match she played and with a 19–2 record against Sharapova many felt she was on course to reach the quarter-finals.

But shortly before the pair were due on court Serena announced she would not be able to play. She had injured a muscle in her chest during her previous match and was having problems hitting her serve. It was a huge disappointment, but Serena knew it was the sensible thing to do. With two more slams to come in 2018 she did not want to risk being out of action for too long.

It was a bump in a road that she always knew would not be entirely smooth. And she was completely honest about those bumps because she knew that the challenges she was facing were not so different to any other working mum. In her pre-Wimbledon press conference, she spoke about the tears she shed when she stopped breastfeeding Olympia, how she felt about missing her daughter's first steps because she was training and how difficult she had found it getting back in shape since giving birth.

But none of that was going to stop her.

At Wimbledon, she proved that to the world by winning six matches in a row to reach the final. She fought hard against two-times Grand Slam winner Angelique Kerber, but could not quite get the better of her. It was a disappointing defeat, but as she said, she was just getting started.

By making it to a Grand Slam final in her fourth tournament back, just ten months after giving birth she had shown that whatever obstacles were put in her way it didn't matter – she'd keep crushing them like she always had done.

She told *Vogue* magazine a few months after Olympia's arrival.

# "I'M SO GLAD I HAD A DAUGHTER. I WANT TO TEACH HER THAT THERE ARE NO LIMITS."

If there is one thing that the career of Serena Williams shows, it is exactly that.

# TIMELINE OF SERENA WILLIAMS'S LIFE

**1981** Born in Michigan

**1985** Starts playing tennis with sister Venus and parents Oracene and Richard in Compton, California.

**1991** The Williams family move to Florida where Venus and Serena train at Rick Macci's tennis academy.

**1995** Plays her first professional tournament in Quebec City, losing 6–1, 6–1 to Annie Miller. Doesn't play another tournament until...

**1997** Wins first main draw match at Ameritech Cup in Chicago and becomes lowest ranked player to defeat two top-ten players in one tournament.

**1998** Plays in her first Grand Slam at the Australian Open.

**1999** Wins first Grand Slam singles title at US Open.

**2000** Serena and Venus become the first sisters to win Olympic gold in doubles tennis.

**2001** Plays in the first ever women's US Open final to be moved to prime-time Saturday night.

**2002** Wins the French Open, Wimbledon and US Open and becomes the first African-American since Althea Gibson to end the year as World Number One.

**2003** Wins the Australian Open to complete her first "Serena Slam".

**2009** Wins tenth Grand Slam singles title at the Australian Open.

**2010** Injury and ill health rule her out for almost a year, causing her ranking to drop outside of the top 100.

**2012** Wins first Olympic singles title and starts working with new coach Patrick Mouratoglou.

**2013** Returns to World Number One, becoming the oldest woman in the Open Era to hold the ranking.

**2015** Wins her nineteenth Grand Slam singles title, surpassing Chris Evert and Martina

Navratilova to move equal third on the list of most Grand Slam singles titles won.

**2016** Wins her twenty-second Grand Slam singles title at Wimbledon, equaling Steffi Graf's record.

**2017** At the Australian Open she wins number twenty-three, surpassing Graf's record and later revealing she did so while pregnant.

**2018** Returns to the tour after having daughter Olympia, playing her first Grand Slam back at the French Open.

**2020** Wins first singles title as a mother at the Auckland Open.

# ABOUT THE AUTHOR

Sarah Shephard has worked in sports journalism for the last 14 years, spending a decade of that as a writer and features editor for *Sport* magazine. While there, she worked on a range of sports including tennis, athletics and football and was fortunate enough to cover three Olympic Games. In recent years, she has worked at *The Times* and helped to launch the football website, *The Coaches' Voice*.

She now covers boxing and football for *The Athletic* and is the author of four books including: *Kicking Off: How Women in Sport are Changing the Game* and the inspirational story of Ruqsana Begum, *Born Fighter*.

# GLOSSARY

**Amateur (in sporting terms):** an athlete who competes without being paid for it or receiving prize money.

**Break (of serve):** when a player wins a game in which their opponent is serving.

**Career Grand Slam:** a player having won all major tournaments at least once in their playing career.

**Changeover:** when players switch sides at pre-determined times during a match. They are allowed a 90 second rest each time, except at the end of a set, when the rest is extended to two minutes.

**Civil rights movement (USA):** a decades-long struggle by African-Americans to end legalised racial discrimination and racial segregation in the USA.

**Code violation:** a rule break called by the umpire which results in the player receiving an official warning or penalty.

**Confederate Flag:** flag representing the Confederacy which was a group of southern states in the American Civil War that fought to keep slavery.

**Drop shot:** a delicate shot where the ball lands just over the net.

**Double fault:** if a player's second serve lands outside of the service box or doesn't clear the net it's a double fault and they lose the point.

**Economic boycott:** when people refuse to buy a certain product, do business with a certain company or spend their money in a certain location.

**Fault:** when a player serves, if the ball lands outside of the service box or doesn't clear the net it's a fault. If this happens on a player's first serve they get a second serve.

**Grand Slam:** the Grand Slam tournaments are the four most important annual tennis events. They include the Australian Open, French Open, US Open and Wimbledon. The term 'Grand Slam' also refers to the achievement of a player winning all four major championships within a calendar year.

**Hawk-eye:** a computer system used in various sports to track the movement of a ball and show its most likely path.

**Jehovah's Witness:** a religious group who use the name 'Jehovah' to refer to God.

**Kingdom Hall:** a place of worship used by Jehovah's Witnesses.

**NAACP:** the National Association for the Advancement of Coloured People is a civil rights organisation in the USA formed in 1909 whose vision is to ensure a society in which all individuals have equal rights without discrimination based on race.

**Open era:** the period in tennis since 1968 when professionals were allowed to compete in Grand Slam tournaments. Before then, only amateurs were allowed to compete for Grand Slam titles.

**Press conference:** a meeting between the media and a player when the media are given time to ask a player questions.

**Professional (in sporting terms):** an athlete who receives payment for their performance.

**Racial segregation:** the systemic separation of people into racial or other ethnic groups in daily life.

**Seeding:** the system used to separate the top players in a draw so that they will not meet in the early rounds of a tournament. Usually the seedings match players' rankings, but some tournaments also take other factors into account when deciding on seeds.

**Segregation:** the action of separating someone or something from others.

**Serena Slam:** being the reigning champion of all four Grand Slam tournaments at the same time, but not all the tournaments have occurred in the same calendar year.

**Sponsor:** a person or organisation that provides financial support.

**Tennis academy:** a kind of school that is focused on tennis. Some academies allow players to stay on site and also provide educational facilities.

**Tennis clinic:** a coaching session or series of sessions.

**Tiebreak:** the way a set is decided if the score in games reaches 6–6.

**Transatlantic slave trade:** the transportation of between 10 and 12 million enslaved Africans across the Atlantic Ocean to North and South America from the 16th to 19th century.

**United States Tennis Association (USTA):** the national governing body for tennis in the USA.

**Wild-card:** a tournament entry awarded to a player at the discretion of the organisers.

**WTA:** the Women's Tennis Association is the main organising body of women's professional tennis and governs the WTA Tour. It was founded in 1973 by Billie Jean King.

# BIBLIOGRAPHY AND FURTHER READING

Angelou, Maya (1995)
*The Complete Collected Poems of Maya Angelou*
Little, Brown Book Group

Williams, Serena (2010)
*My Life: Queen of the Court*
Simon & Schuster UK

Williams, Serena and Williams, Venus (2005)
*Venus & Serena: Serving from the Hip*
Houghton Mifflin

# INDEX